Roger and **Janette Klopfenstein** had traveled from their Ohio home to a Wisconsin clinic where Rog was seeking help for headaches which resulted from a form of muscular dystrophy. To the other guests at the motel where they stayed, the family may have seemed like any other young parents with two small sons. Those who watched Rog closely could tell that he moved more slowly, shuffled slightly, and had to support himself when sitting or rising.

Those who knew him intimately noticed that for the past three months he was constantly tired and more weak. But no one would have guessed that this twenty-nine-year old father would simply stop breathing during a nap in their motel room. There was no way of knowing that the muscles of Rog's diaphragm had so deteriorated that oxygen was no longer being supplied to his body.

To Janette and the boys, the death was as sudden and unexpected as any accidental death. In her first book, *My Walk Through Grief* (Herald Press, 1976), Janette shares her personal pilgrimage through the emotional and social problems of losing a husband to death. This second book, *Tell Me About Death, Mommy*, deals with her experiences in helping her sons understand and cope with death.

Tell Me
About Death,
Mommy

Janette Klopfenstein

Introduction by
J. Lorne Peachey

HERALD PRESS
Scottdale, Pennsylvania
Kitchener, Ontario

TELL ME ABOUT DEATH, MOMMY
Copyright © 1977 by Herald Press, Scottdale, Pa. 15683
   Published simultaneously in Canada, by Herald Press,
   Kitchener, Ont. N2G 4M5
Library of Congress Catalog Card Number: 77-76989
International Standard Book Number: 0-8361-1821-9
Printed in the United States of America
Design: Alice B. Shetler

To Chad and Dereck, who cooperated
  in the writing of this book.
May you remember that these
  personal things were shared
To help other children who must
  face the pain of death.

Contents

Introduction

Part of my work as a family magazine editor is reading unsolicited manuscripts from writers who want to be published. Often the task becomes discouraging as I reject manuscript after manuscript because it doesn't have anything to say or doesn't say it well.

But I keep on reading, dozens of submissions each week, because I know that somewhere in that stack is just the article I need: well-written, logical thinking, practical suggestions, saying something in a way not quite said before. And it may just be from a new writer.

That was my experience in the spring of 1974. The subject: death. The writer: Janette Klopfenstein. "How to Help in Time of Death," which appeared in the August 1974 issue of *Christian Living*, was Janette's first published work.

From that beginning Janette has gone on to write other articles and her first book, *My Walk Through Grief*. Now she has written *Tell Me About Death, Mommy*, with the same candor and honesty about her experiences and feelings that marked her earlier work. In it she suggests ways parents can help their children work through the traumas associated with death.

Death, like sex, is a subject many parents find difficult to discuss with their children. So many unknowns lurk in our own minds, so many questions in theirs. And, if adults would admit it, few of us like to think about of our own mortality.

Tell Me About Death, Mommy, first of all, forced me to think through my own ideas and feelings about death. My children should eventually benefit. For before I can help them understand death, I must come to terms with it myself. And like in so many areas, what my children finally come to think and believe about death will be strongly influenced by what they see modeled by my wife, Emily, and me.

Janette writes out of personal experience. In a motel room far from home she lost her husband while her two young sons looked on. After the funeral, the initial shock, and the outpouring of grief, the boys asked many questions.

Those questions are here. So are Janette's answers—simple, practical, positive. While some may quarrel with specific answers, none can argue with the author's willingness to deal seriously with this subject.

For those who are young, death seems far away. Yet, from the moment of birth, it begins to touch our lives. What all of us must realize, and help our children to understand, is that only as we come to terms with death are we able to live. *Tell Me About Death, Mommy* helps us do both.

J. Lorne Peachey, Editor
Christian Living Magazine

Author's
Preface

"Is daddy going to be all right?" Six-year-old Chad's question hung heavy that warm August day when I returned to the motel room from which his father's body had been hurriedly removed. I stood in the long, dark hall, dazed beyond belief by what the last hours had brought. My frantic attempt to awaken Rog from a nap, the sickening pit in my being when I realized he wasn't breathing, the long, hopeless ambulance trip to the hospital, and the tiresome, repetitive description of his death to a stream of medical people had thrown me into an unfamiliar, disarrayed world. Calling back to our Ohio home with the shocking news and being escorted back to the motel room alone seemed completely unreal.

I saw Chad and three-year-old Dereck come running from the sitter. Chad's tug on my arm and his innocent, concerned face looking up at me with hope pulled me out of my daze. I looked at him and his question broke my heart.

How could I say, "Daddy is dead"? How does one tell a happy six-year-old, who loves his father in the most admiring way, that daddy will never again play ball, greet him at the door after a day of work, or share the joy of his fun? How should I say to a three-year-old that daddy will no longer be here to tuck him in bed, fix his toys, or snuggle him in warm arms? How do we ever say, "Someone you loved very much is dead!"

This book is an attempt to share what I have learned about children and death from our very personal, tragic experience and from the interaction I have had with groups of children. Discussing death with a child is so difficult that we naturally want to resist. Yet we know that to wait until death occurs makes giving general explanations too unbearably painful. Ideally our child should have some concepts and answers to draw upon when he comes to an intimate experience with death.

In the last part of this book I share specific things that succeeded in helping the boys face the death of their father. I also include some of the failures I had in understanding a child's grief process and adjustment. This is done with the hope that those who are relating to a bereaved child may find encouragement as well as practical suggestions to help that child deal with death. I speak to all parents and adults as well, because thinking about death now may make reactions during a time of crisis more rational. Being aware may allow us to be less overpowered by the heavy emotions which surround death.

Perhaps nothing can prepare a child for the emotional loss of separation from someone he loves. However, by giving the child some basic concepts and by understanding his needs, we can lessen the trauma and help him better cope with death.   *Janette Klopfenstein*

1
Please
Don't Ask Me
About Death!

"Mommy, what does it mean to die?" My first attempt at explaining death to a child came long before I was personally involved with death. Although Rog and I discussed our feelings openly, talking about death always left me a bit shaken and very melancholy. Trying to sort things out in my own mind was hard enough, but when our first son, Chad, started asking questions, I realized the difficulty of making death understandable to a child.

Chad's question caused me to do a lot of stammering. I recall on those first occasions muttering some theological terms which hardly seemed appropriate for his young years. As I would escape from the bedside, where Chad always seemed to have his deep thoughts, I'd sigh and tell Rog that I really didn't think a three-year-old needed to know about death. Why did our son have to be so inquisitive!

I was all prepared to tell Chad about sex and prided myself on the honest way we had recently handled the birth of his baby brother. Educated by the many books written on the correct way to answer any question, I waited and gave appropriate information for his age. However, questions about death were another matter. My generation which had become so liberated about discussing the beginning of life had little experience and no familiarity with explaining the ending of life.

Not only was I unprepared and uneducated to answer a child's questions about death, but I also had a strong urge to protect Chad from the unpleasant aspects of life. I really didn't *want* to explain death to an innocent, fun-loving little boy! Conceiving childhood as a time of joy and idyllic existence—a time when all is well with the world—I hated the thought of telling him that life also includes tragedy and death.

My own childhood memories of warmth, many friends, little conflict, and no memorable crisis fed my dream that the young years should be a happy experience rather than a time of concern about adult things such as death. Consequently, I hoped to build a shell of love around Chad to allow him to grow up unthreatened by fear and problems. He deserved a childhood just like mine! So when he began quietly asking what it means to die, I instinctively wanted to say, "Chad, please don't ask me about that. You're too young to be aware that people die."

Along with my idealistic, maternal desire to protect Chad, I had an uncanny belief that if we'd ignore the subject of death, maybe we'd never have to face it—at least not for a long time. Maybe we'd be fortunate and our happiness would continue forever! Embracing the positive experiences of life with gusto and shoving under the table the negative aspects of living, I had built quite a paragon of happiness.

My teen and college years with their good times and serious academic pursuit had built a good base. The self-fulfillment of teaching along with achievement and approval in many areas added to the structured happiness of "everything going right" for me. Then marriage brought a good, caring husband, healthy children, and much success. We were involved deeply in church and community. My life fit the mold as if it had been ordered out of an American dream catalog.

Sometimes I'd get frightened inside, worrying that my rose garden life couldn't go on forever. Usually I just held to the belief that well-being would always be available to anyone who cared as much as I. At the top of my list of goals, verbalized at retreats and in group encounters, I always gave "happiness" top priority. The height of fulfillment and extreme satisfaction came when Rog wrote, "You've made this the happiest year of my life," on an anniversary card.

Neither death nor disease fit into my concept of the good life and to have a child repeatedly bring up the subject was a bit annoying.

Then we discovered that Rog's longtime weakness was a form of muscular dystrophy which would progress with no possible cure. Rog refused to shatter my dreams and minimized the disease by periodically reassuring me that the specialist had said deterioration would be slow. Happiness and good relationships became even more cherished. Although I usually tried to ignore an unknown future, my New Year's prayer each year always seemed to be, "Just let the next year be as happy as the last one."

Chad was nearly four when we learned of Rog's disease. Because the weakness was observable only to those who "knew" and because we expected the loss of strength to be very gradual, we saw no reason to worry Chad. When his father stopped breathing that August day in the motel room, Chad had no idea that Rog had any kind of illness. We had indeed protected him.

Fortunately, Chad had not allowed me to ignore his questions about death. Those early, sporadic young questions had intensified over the next several years. Frequently Chad had insisted on discussing death, quizzing and challenging my answers. The decision to be honest had eventually outweighed my propensity to protect and ignore. Even though I approached the subject in an academic, impersonal way, by the time he was six, Chad had caught some basic concepts about death.

When he came running with his question, "Is daddy going to be all right?" I felt a distinct and gratifying relief that Chad had forced me to overcome the natural resistance which had tried to keep me from discussing death. A tape clicked in my mind. I could repeat words of explanation which I had given in a time when I was not emotionally and intellectually blinded by death's painful reality.

2
When
Should I Tell
What?

Now I know that Chad's soft plea, "Tell me about death, Mommy," was a normal part of childhood. He was not necessarily a precocious child or a worry wart when he started being concerned about death at age three. No amount of protecting can insulate a child from thoughts about death. As parents we can count on the fact that at some age our child will want to know about death, whether or not he can or will verbalize his feelings.

The time at which the questions begin depends on the personality of the child or on the exposure he has had to death. Explaining death to a child should come when he is interested and ready. It should not be forced upon him simply because some "authority" says that by such and such an age a child should know certain prescribed facts. Understanding death doesn't work that way.

Death can be a frightening and worrisome subject to a child. Explaining it must be done at his own level of understanding and concern. As parents it is hard not to compare one child's awareness with another's. Just because Chad was asking all those detailed questions about death didn't mean that my friend Mary Ann's child of the same age was ready for or interested in the same information. When I shared that Chad was challenging me with such deep questions for his age, I remember that she was tempted to push her three-year-old daughter, Audra, into thinking about death also. Fortunately she didn't.

Some books on the subject of death try to chart an age graph of a child's awareness. Parents eagerly read the chart, hoping to find when to tell what information about death. Some books say that by age three a child can understand that death happens. Not until age five can he understand that it is final and then by age seven or so he can accept that it is universal—that it will happen to everyone including himself. Such general statements may be interesting, but all such efforts at categorizing children always end by saying each child is an individual who varies in thinking, in his needs, and in his experiences with death.

Some young children seem able to grasp the abstract, spiritual concepts of death while others find it more difficult. Some children seem to have more curiosity or anxiety about the unknown. For some children, seeing a sad movie or hearing about a death may prompt a flood of questions and concerns. Other children may need a more direct encounter with death to care about knowing. Our second son, Dereck, was more carefree and less sensitive as a small child. Although he was nearly four when Rog died, he had previously shown no interest in the subject. Even though he heard Chad and me talk about death, he never asked questions or probed for answers.

The parent who knows the personality of the child and his individual situation can best judge when a child should be told about death. The parent who intimately feels where a child is in his development can best decide what information he is able to understand at this time. Sometimes, as in Dereck's case, a very young child is forced to understand death because it has become part of his life.

3
The Need
Behind the
Question

At the first mention of the word death from the child's lips, some informed, honest parents who abhor evasiveness sit the child on a chair and inform him, "You've shown an interest in death. Okay, I'm going to explain it to you." By the third well-expressed sentence the parent completely loses the child's attention. The truth is that the child doesn't really want a lecture on death.

Unless he has been personally touched by the death of a young friend, a child generally understands death as happening to others—usually older people—and not to himself. Consequently, when he first expresses a desire to know about death, it is usually not out of concern about his own death. Detailed explanations about the nature of death don't really answer his needs.

When a child has learned by experience or has been told by someone that death is different from going on vacation or moving away—that it is a final thing from which no one returns—he may be faced with great fear. Although he still plays "shoot 'em dead" followed by getting up and doing it again, he knows that in real life such fantasy doesn't happen. When the foreverness of death settles on a child's mind, he has all kinds of worries with which to deal.

A child may begin by asking general questions such as, "What happens when people die?" or by making broad statements like, "Tell me about death." But it is to the worries behind the questions that parents must direct their first answers about death.

In the child's young eyes his parents seem old. The young thought that people die when they get old and that perhaps his parents are going to die too is so frightening that he may be unable to express his fears and the awful feeling inside.

What he desperately wants to know is, "What will happen to me if Mommy or Daddy die? Who will take care of me if Mom or Dad go away forever?" Often those questions are too painful for a child to ask. Instead he may do a lot of quiet worrying, building a horrible picture in his mind.

Discerning why a child is asking about death is as important as having all the right words ready. Holding the child with a caring, listening attitude may reveal whether he wants to discuss death or just needs reassurance of continued care. Instead of immediately using the opportunity to teach our child concepts about death, we can feel him out with such questions as, "Why do you ask?" or "Are you worried that someone may die?" or "What do you think might happen?"

According to several studies, nearly 80 percent of a child's fears center around death. Most of these fears have to do with being left alone or no onger having the love of one of the parents. Children of our friends who had shown little interest in death before, suddenly began asking a lot of questions and stating many fears after seeing Chad and Dereck lose a father. The biggest concern was not so much what happens at death as it was a projection of our situation onto themselves. What would happen to them if their mommy or daddy died too?

When a child is asking questions about death from that standpoint, he first of all needs assurance that mother and father hope to be here to take care of him for a long time. He needs to be told how much his parents love him and how they enjoy being here to raise him. Telling the child that we're not going to die of old age for a long time and helping him understand time and age may relax him. If our child has seen a friend's parent die, he should be told the cause of death. Knowing that such an illness or such an accident is rare will keep him from constantly worrying that parents suddenly die for no apparent reason.

For the child who is troubled about the death of a parent, assurance of our love may not be enough. He may need some concrete clarification about what actually would happen to him in case of a parent's death. Can a child somehow catch from his family life that either parent would be strong enough to care for him alone if the other parent died? Can we tell our child with confidence that a group of friends and relatives would surround our family if mommy or daddy died? Are there men who would step in as father images if daddy died and women we could count on to provide some mothering if mommy died?

If we are a mobile family, living away from relatives and having to adapt to new areas every several years, surrounding ourselves with stable friendships and providing caring adults to relate to our children may be more difficult. The concept of the larger, extended family living near to help each other has been replaced by the isolated, nuclear family trying to exist alone. When death comes into our families today, the void is devastating because often the needed emotional support and physical help are lacking.

If our child cannot feel a natural group which he knows would readily give care and concern, we should make an effort to provide "adopted" aunt, uncle, grandparent, and adult friend figures—people the child knows he could turn to for love and attention. Many families are finding such figures in the church community or in family-oriented small groups who make commitments of support to each other.

The thought of being orphaned by the death of both parents is, of course, the most horrible thought of all and the one about which a child often worries the most. Many children secretly wonder and draw up fantasies about where they would live and what they would do. As a little girl, I had decided which aunt and uncle would be the best parents to me. I imagined how I would fit into their family and pictured a good life with them. Although I never verbalized my ideas to my parents, having my choice settled in my mind gave me a lot of security.

Many parents show their wills to the children or explain who has been chosen as guardian. Much worry can be alleviated and dreadful fabrications avoided if a child knows that someone has offered and sincerely wants to provide a home for him; he would not be left alone. To understand exactly where he would fit in and to know that he would be loved by guardians who already take a great interest in him may answer many of his present questions about death.

Being aware of why our child is asking about death will make us sensitive about giving him what he needs at the time.

4
Opening
Possibilities
for Sharing

Not all children who have a need and are concerned about death are willing to open a discussion or express questions about death. Many worry and fret in silence. A mother recently related that her outgoing, friendly daughter became sullen and difficult in school after the death of a baby brother. Fortunately the teacher was a widowed mother who recognized the child's hidden fears and questions. When the mother realized that the little girl's silence about the death did not mean understanding and acceptance, she opened up discussion. After several talks the child seemed to relax and regain her personality.

When a child is going through a difficult emotional time and we can't seem to place our finger on the cause, perhaps he needs to hear us ask, "Is anything bothering or worrying you?" It may be that the mental pictures of death conjured up by a frightened child's mind are exhibiting themselves in unfamiliar behavior and personality changes. If that is the case, we may have to be prepared to listen at length until the child summons enough courage to talk about his death thoughts.

Sometimes a child cannot even name the feeling which is causing the anxiety, the upset stomach, and the possessive way he feels about those he loves. Because he has never heard his parents discuss death, he isn't aware that his frustration may be death-related. He only knows that when he sees people die on the evening news or hears about the death of someone in the community, he feels scared inside. He needs parents who will first of all help him identify his feelings before he can begin expressing himself. If our child seems overly anxious about being alone, about going to sleep, or about being separated from us, we can try to get him to share by opening the conversation. We can ask, "Is something frightening you?" or "Does something worry you before you go to sleep?" or "What do you think might happen if we go away?"

How do we prepare openings and provide occasions for the reticent child to discuss death without being too blunt or too forceful in asking him to share his worries? By trying to draw out the child, don't we take the chance of upsetting him, pressuring him to discuss something he isn't ready to share?

The possibility of burdening the child with too

much stress in getting him to talk is of course very real. As I'm writing this I can imagine all the parent readers gasping at the possible fears and worries about death that may be hidden in their child's mind. I envision them putting down this book and with determination hunting down the child so that they can phrase a question or give an opening so their child will discuss death. Gentle questioning of a worried child is one thing, but insisting he tell where he is in his feelings about death rarely works.

Ideally, discussion about death should emerge from a natural situation. As parents we can simply be aware of appropriate times and take advantage of such opportunities in a matter-of-fact way. There are many ordinary circumstances when death can easily be mentioned. Talking about the order of the seasons, the seeds in the ground, and other phenomena of nature dying provide obvious ways. Initiating a sharing about feelings in a sad movie or reading a story about death are good ways to approach the subject. Bedtime or quiet times often bring out things that need to be said. If we don't want to get into a deep discussion right before sleeping, we can at least take cues about what our child is thinking and bring it up another time. Letting the child know that we too have emotions about death is a natural way to set the stage for him to share his feelings freely.

How much better to begin discussion when we can have a calm setting for sharing. When I stood in that motel hall with Chad asking me about his father, I was so dazed and bewildered that I could not have explained anything to him rationally. Thank goodness we had discussed death in a general, matter-of-fact, impersonal way and I could recall the exact words I had said before.

The best and most natural way I've found to talk about death with a child is to talk about life. As we share with our child how much we value life and appreciate the experiences we enjoy, we can also mention that life doesn't last forever. We can begin to use phrases like "life on this earth" or "the time we have on earth" to help our child understand that we conceive life here as something that ends. We can share our belief that this time is given to us to use productively, to serve others and to enjoy. If we see life here as transient—the "now" of eternity—we can give our child both an appreciation for the value of life and an understanding that this part will end.

Before any major explanation or exposure to death occurs, the Christian parent wants his child to have a solid base of knowing God's love. Our children learn about this love not only from what they hear us say but from how they see us reacting—whether we really value and experience God's love affecting our lives. Do our children see us viewing God's love as a magic protection blanket which should keep us from harm and danger and provide only good in this world? Or do they sense that we have a trust and assurance of His love being with us through *all* of life? A concept of God as the Great Magician or Fairy God Mother who is there only to call on for our wishes and our protection hardly holds up in a time of crisis. I want my children to see God as a source of greatest love, always there no matter what happens.

Let's look at our prayers with our children. If they always run, "Keep us safe. Keep us from harm. Don't let this or that happen," the child may be learning to expect that kind of reaction from God. How much better to communicate the idea of God's love as eternal, unchanging, and deeply caring regardless of what happens. I want my child to hear prayers such as, "God, help us to know that You are with us through the good and the bad," and later, "God, give us the confidence to know that You take care of us in our life and in our death." The idea of God's love "always being there" prepares a child for learning about the reality and the facts of death more than any other concept. I want Chad and Dereck to see God's love as the one permanent entity.

Along with giving our child natural occasions to share and a background of general concepts about life and God's love, we can also allow him some general exposure and experience with the reality of death. Because children of my parent's generation were frequently involved in death situations, dying was an obvious part of life for them.

Today our children live in a paradoxical relationship with death. On the one hand they are bombarded with death on television and in newspapers, but on the other hand they are almost completely isolated from personal involvement with death. Because of the deluge of violence and death in the media it would seem that our children would be quite familiar with it.

However, our children seem to be able to shrug off such death as just another crime or police story. Today firsthand exposure to death has nearly been eliminated from a child's experience. The terminally ill are removed to modern hospitals where children aren't allowed to visit. Our retirement homes separate old age death from the child's world. Funeral homes remove most of the burial rituals from the home. Children do not seem to fit into the quiet solemn atmosphere.

Death always happens "out there" in some vague place and manner. A child feels no familiar connection with it at all. When someone's death is discussed, it is often in hushed tones meant only for adult ears. The secrecy, the aura of silence, and the let's-not-involve-the-children attitude makes death frightening and mysterious because children are forced to draw their own ideas about what is really involved.

Yet parents today generally feel that having death removed from the main stream of living is much better. In a strong reaction to the past when children were sometimes forced to witness hysterical emotions and even made to do such things as unwillingly kiss the corpse of someone they loved, our generation tends to dissociate death from life. Explaining death to a child may be necessary, we say, but allowing him to be exposed to "real" death is not often advocated.

I feel that a child who has had some contact with the reality of death will have a better understanding if death tragically interrupts his life. Instead of keeping news of a death in the community from him, we can share some of our thoughts and feelings about death. We can use such death incidents to show that sadness and tears are a normal part of facing death. A child who has been encouraged to show sympathy— "We feel sad that it happened"—and express his feelings about another person's loss—"How do you think he feels?"—will be better able to get in touch with his own feelings of grief and bereavement when he faces a close death.

If a child expresses interest in going to the funeral home and "seeing" death for himself, what should we say? Having read about the terrible trauma caused by forcing a child to view a corpse, I generally held the view that children shouldn't be taken to funeral homes. However, when Chad was five he became very curious about what a corpse looked like and asked a lot of questions about the body. At that time Rog's elderly great-aunt died and a small family funeral was arranged. We allowed Chad to attend. A lot of his curiosity was satisfied and it wasn't at all traumatic. It was good that Chad had some knowledge of caskets and a corpse before he saw his father's body. I'm not advocating taking our children with us to all death situations, but perhaps a limited exposure, especially if requested by the child, may help both in explaining death and in his future experiences with death.

Another form of contact with death that our child may experience is the loss of a loved pet. Although losing a dog in no way compares with the death of a family member or loved friend, some of the feelings are the same. Such losses can give the child a small dose of some of the reactions and pain surrounding death and can provide a good base for discussion.

The way the death of a pet is handled may cause the child to draw certain conclusions about death. First of all, he learns of death's finality. If his feelings of loss are respected and he is allowed to cry and express sadness, he learns that it is okay to feel that way about death. If he is laughed at, told to be brave, or hears death minimized with, "Oh, it was just an old dog anyway," he learns that love feelings aren't important and shouldn't be shown or expressed.

What does a child learn when he is told not to be sad, because we will go out and buy a new pet right away? If he's consoled, allowed to help bury the pet, and encouraged to recall good things about his animal, he learns that death does have severe consequences. Love cannot always be immediately replaced. After a time, when he is ready to love again, he will appreciate a new pet.

Providing opportunities for a child to share his thoughts about death should be natural and free. However, such a treatment of death is not always easy.

5
All That
Sounds Nice
But . . .

All this talk about treating death matter-of-factly and being open and helpful in exposing our child to experiences that draw out discussion sounds very nice and sensible. We would like to be the super cool parent who can handle death with finesse—one who calmly uses situations lovingly to teach a child and help him with his fears.

The problem is that most of us, if we're honest, haven't really come to grips with death ourselves. How am I to tell my child confidently about death when I haven't worked much beyond my own childhood fears, fantasies, and defenses against the reality of death?

Some of us have learned to build such a block against death that we have trained ourselves not to think about it. We're young and our children are healthy. It won't happen to us! We can't be bothered by thoughts of death and grief. Those who have left no room for building a concept of death face a terrible crash when death breaks through the defenses and must be faced as a personally tragic happening.

Many of us, however, struggle long and hard with death. Although I had been reticent about discussing death with Chad and although death didn't really fit into my well-structured, happy life picture, thoughts of death often came thundering into my mind. Consequently Rog and I had done a lot of sharing as I tried to work out my vague and frightening worries.

Even as an adult, thinking about my own death always left me empty and scared. I was so involved in life that I really couldn't identify with Christians who talked about death as "leading to the better land" or "freeing us from trials." Immortality and heaven represented such an unknown; I had to admit that I wasn't at all sure it could measure up to the life I was experiencing here.

Even more than wondering and worrying about the meaning of life after death, I just could not conceive of myself not being here in the little world we had built. To think of missing the fun, having someone else mother the boys, or Rog choosing another wife left me depressed. I knew it was a selfish feeling, but it was very real. My serious concern was hid by the humorous plea to Rog, "If I die, you'd better at least mourn me for a year." I couldn't tolerate the thought of being forgotten. When I observed a death and saw the community praise the bereaved family for "getting back to living" or "getting over" the death as quickly as possible, I shuddered. To think my death would be so hurriedly minimized made death seem unbearable.

Rog, on the other hand, seemed to accept peacefully the inevitability of his own death. He seemed to have few hangups about honestly wanting us to rebuild a good life without him. "One has to accept tragedy," he would say. "When there's nothing else to do, we must decide to go on and make a good life." Calmly he'd say, "Your remarriage would be a compliment to me—a sign that you feel marriage is good," or "If anything happens to me I want you to be financially free to raise the boys alone. I want you to marry out of love not need." The way Rog accepted death and the restructuring of a new life sometimes nearly drove me to distraction. I kept thinking that he'd probably cope well if I died. Even though I knew he was being wiser and more sensible, I always considered it inconceivable that life could go on without me.

How can we tell a child about death when we haven't accepted it ourselves? Our children obviously have enough fears of their own without being saddled with ours too.

Having a caring husband to whom I could express any kind of fear or feeling helped me. Even though our views differed, he listened while I worked through my worries. I also had several close friends with whom I shared my struggles about death. I did much reading and searching for answers throughout my adult years. It helped to know that countless people, including the most devout, have wrestled with fears of death.

However, some people may need a more specific type of help. If the fear of our own death becomes overwhelming and controlling, we should definitely seek some solid professional and spiritual counseling in understanding our insecure feelings. A friend of mine went through a year when she just "knew" she was going to die. First she felt she had heart trouble and when that was not so, she convinced herself it was probably cancer. She was living with two small sons and a busy husband in a new town, far from friends and relatives with whom to share her apprehension. As she looks back now at that year she counts it wasted, ruined by the fear which controlled her and made her unable to function normally. She needed help.

For many adults the possibility of being widowed is even more dreaded than personal death. How can we calmly handle our child's fear of losing love and being left alone when the same worries plague us? Many men and women have told me, "I just hope I go first because I couldn't go on without my partner."

Women especially greatly fear being widowed and many believe that surviving without a husband would scarcely be possible. Such fear is not completely irrational because they have observed the way many widowed persons seem to be ostracized by society or become social dropouts by their own choosing.

For the mother of our now-typical small family structure, the fear of losing a child can be as great as the fear of losing a spouse. The death of a child shatters a mother's world. She cannot turn her attention to a number of other children who need her as bereaved mothers of previous generations could.

Help! What are we to do with these natural fears of death and how can we possibly explain death to our children when we are still struggling with death ourselves? Perhaps, the best place to start is to first of all admit that we have problems with death—either our own death or losing a loved one. The only way to begin to handle our fears is to look at them and talk about them.

Instead of mouthing pious words in Sunday school about how the Christian shouldn't have any problems with death, let's be honest by helping each other face our real feelings. Together maybe we can learn to live—trusting God in spite of our fears. A faith built with regard to our real needs is better than being able to trust because we've smothered all those feelings we think a Christian shouldn't have.

If there is any way to make our own death more acceptable and less frightening to us, it is probably through actually internalizing the belief that the quality of life is more important than the quantity. Living with meaning—making the most of situations and relationships—will make us less concerned about life's length and more concerned about its flavor. Facing up to my own death makes me want to love, to care, and to share while I may. My days become more intensely precious when I accept the uncertainty of their number.

Accepting the inevitability of my death allows me the freedom to discuss my wishes and my concerns about how life should go on when I am no longer here. Being able to say what I would like for my children permits me to worry less about what they will do if I die. Wanting to be remembered or to have some influence over life after we're gone is not morbid unless it becomes possessive and selfish. Making picture albums, movies, mementos, and keepsakes for our children is a natural way of admitting death is a possibility. Some parents find therapeutic value in making recordings or writing letters to be opened at their death.

Admitting our own fears about losing loved ones will certainly make us more compassionate and understanding when our child shares such feeling. Just as he is helped with his fears by knowing that a circle of people care, we as adults can find comfort and security in knowing that there are people who will stand by us if death comes close. We can cultivate friendships and family ties that are deep and lasting. We can be the kind of person who supports others during crisis and we will receive the same when our day comes.

Is it possible to overcome the fear of being widowed? Anyone who knows the deep sharing and loving of another person dreads the ending of that beautiful relationship. We're afraid of being alone. All the social pressures to couple and the barrage of songs with words like, "You are the meaning in my life" and "I can't live without you" and "You are my everything," successfully convince us that we can't make it without a spouse's love. Combating feelings which make us seem empty and lost unless we're married is difficult but necessary if we are working out our fears of death.

If my sole identity is dependent on the position and the partnership of my husband, there is little hope of overcoming an unhealthy fear of his death. Loving one another is a most precious and cherished gift. But to become completely absorbed only in that union—to have no worth on my own and no interest outside what we are as a couple—leaves me vulnerable to fear.

My religious views and beliefs are of prime importance in influencing how I handle and work through my fears of death. What *do* I believe about death?

6
What
Do I Myself Believe
About Death?

"Mommy, what really happens when we die?" When our child moves beyond the point of simply needing reassurance about his fears and is no longer satisfied with the general way we've been mentioning death, we are faced with the enormous task of giving him specific answers.

The statements we make will greatly depend on whether or not we as parents have come to an understanding and have worked out a fairly definite set of beliefs about the meaning of death. Explaining death to a child when we aren't at all sure what we believe ourselves is unsettling. When we're consistently floundering with half-belief and vague concepts, we can't convincingly give our child a satisfying foundation for his belief. If we've dismissed some of our own childhood fantasies but have not gone on and developed mature concepts that we believe, we will probably end up passing on the fantasies even though we know they didn't work for us. Older children especially will detect if we personally believe what we're saying.

Coming to an understanding of what I believe about death has been a long, painful struggle for me. My questioning started as a young girl when I had a hard time believing the fantastic resurrection story. Although I tried hard, I couldn't release my lingering doubt that the whole story of Christ and eternal life was just too supernatural to be true. Even after I had personally accepted Christ and had basically endorsed for my life the values Christ taught, faith never came easy for me.

A church college made me stronger in my values and ideas of service to others, but generally my faith lagged behind and the periodic doubting went deeper. After I had rationalized miracles and explained away the supernatural, I was left pretty much with a Christ who had come to change society—a moral example for me to follow. Yet I knew that was not enough!

Between my times of doubting, which descended sporadically during the next ten years, there were long periods when I experienced a meaningful relationship with God. I accepted Him by faith and believed in the reality of the supernatural. Because I wasn't a strongly vocal or rebellious doubter, my questioning was considered an asset, a means of stirring discussion in Sunday school class. But few people knew how deep my questions went or how much I admired those with a simple faith. At times my mind entertained all kinds of possibilities from the nonexistence of God to the idea that religion was merely a crutch proposed by man to cope with the unpleasant aspects of life.

Rog's death came at a time of fairly stable faith, although I recall doing some bargaining with God when I realized that something was happening to Rog. We both had projected any effects of Rog's illness far into the future. (Someday, a long time from now, his weakness may become serious.) When I observed that he was continually tired, constantly fighting off headaches, and frequently losing his balance, I panicked. I couldn't dismiss it as the flu, which Rog tried to do at first. When the clinic offered the possibility of help, I pleaded with God, "If you'll keep Rog's disease from progressing, I'll never doubt You again." Bargaining to have faith wasn't God's answer for me.

Facing death in such a personal way made me take a good hard look at my doubting. I felt a strong drive to find the TRUTH. I needed desperately to know what I believed about God and about the meaning of immortality. I began a deep search. Perhaps my quest would lead to answers I didn't want to hear, but I knew I could live with truth better than I could live with the thought of just believing whatever made me feel good.

For years I had tried to develop my faith by positive thinking. Or I had tried to suppress intellectual thought to obtain a naiveté which I thought must be necessary for faith. After Rog died, I prayed for a vision or a definable supernatural experience to insure my faith. Finally I realized that, for me, faith had to be a receiving of God's Word with trust. Either I had to believe what Christ says is TRUTH or forever write Him off as a lunatic who claimed to be God's Son. My step out in faith was rewarded by a gentle solidifying of belief and ideas.

I believe God created man as an eternal being to live in harmony with Him. Death resulted because man chose to break communion with God. Christ was sent to restore our connection and to show us that death is not the end, but that we are in fact the eternal beings God intended.

I believe man is both spiritual and physical. My spirit which cares, loves, thinks, feels, and touches God is entwined with my physical existence. Yet this *being* part of me is also somehow separate from my body and my physical life. There is much more to me than can be experienced by the senses. I'm more than my observable life and the Janette which seems obvious to others.

It is this eternal-real part of me, the inner soul/being which Christ came to renew and give supreme attention. We miss so much if we view Christ's coming as only setting up moral examples and social ideals for an earthly kingdom. His disciples were disappointed that He didn't fulfill their expectations until they understood that the inward power which He gave was more valuable than all the most idealistic outward changes imaginable.

When I accept the eternal nature of myself,

the condition of my spirit and its relationship to God and others becomes most important. I start to identify and evaluate myself in relation to where my inner soul/being is at this time instead of judging myself in completely physical terms— how I look, what I've done, or how well I fulfill all the cultural expectations laid before me. Instead of concentrating all my energies on outward things and being concerned where I rank on society's rating chart of acceptability, I begin to catch the vision that my inner being's connection with God's love is vastly more important. All else is temporal. Only what I learn of love will last forever.

Death is not so much a beginning as it is a change. Life on earth is one stage of eternity—a time to learn, to help each other, and to test and to choose. This time on earth is very important. Death cannot suddenly make us "all knowing" if we've neglected to know God while we're here. Although death means the total end of physical living, for my being it is an immediate, unexplainable transition of my relationship with God into another realm of experience. I will be involved in a higher form of existence and continue in dimensions of growth and stages of knowledge which my mind cannot even fathom now.

All this is extremely mystical and hard to conceive for one who is as earthbound as I. The Bible gives assurance that the "I" is somehow separate from the body at death. "Then shall the dust return to the earth as it was: and the spirit shall return unto God who gave it" (Ecclesiastes

12:7) or "Fear not them which kill the body, but are not able to kill the soul" (Matthew 10:28).

During my search I read many accounts written by people who could have been declared clinically dead but were revived by unusual medical means. The writers tell of leaving the body and an indescribable feeling of movement toward some kind of peacefulness and light.

I've personally shared with a friend who had an experience of approaching heaven during a coma caused by a tragic car accident. She recalls so much joy and peace and has shared the encouraging words, "I know this is difficult to understand, but I'm not afraid to die, because I've had a taste of the experience."

Dr. Elizabeth Kubler-Ross, author of *On Death and Dying*, was convinced that existence terminated at the grave until she worked with thousands of dying patients. Now she is certain that only the physical body dies and that psychic life goes on. She says, "None of the patients who have had a death experience and returned are ever afraid to die. At first there is an experience of floating out of the body, a separation of oneself from the corpse."

To know that immortality will be better than those moments when I have already felt the eternal is great. The part of me that feels stable even when all else around me is fluctuating, the part of me that sometimes touches another person in a spiritual, completely unphysical way, and that part of me that at times can feel peace in spite of unbearable circumstances—that part of me never dies.

46

7

How
Do I Put That into
Child's Language?

In the weeks that followed Rog's death, the children who were close to us—friends and cousins of Chad and Dereck—had much to say about death. Their confusion was evident when I overheard their child conversation. Their Christian parents had tried to give them a perspective of death which showed great faith ("Rog is with Jesus now"). Not only had the children received instruction at home but they had been well taught in Sunday school. All the children seemed to have an unquestioning acceptance that death meant going to heaven.

However, the parents and teachers had not been effective in helping the child to understand the separation of our being from our physical bodies. Consequently, the children who attended the burial service had to come up with their own answers to overcome the contradiction of wanting to believe that Rog was in heaven and yet seeing him dead in the casket.

One little boy said, "Rog is in heaven. He must have jumped out before they closed the casket." Another thought he had a better answer. Since he hadn't seen the casket lowered into the grave, he knew that "Jesus sneaked in and opened the lid to let Rog out before the gravemen put it into the hole."

One cousin tried to convince Chad and Dereck that an angel had come and carried the casket to the clouds and that it is floating around up there in heaven somewhere. Chad had little success in trying to explain to his friends, who had been given no concept of the distinction between the being and the body, that "Daddy is in heaven; only his body is in the grave."

Dereck firmly denied statements made by his friends, because he knew better. I heard him say, "The casket is in the ground. Jesus didn't come and open the lid!" However, he showed his own lack of understanding when I heard him tell someone on the telephone, "My daddy's head is in the graveyard. His feet are in heaven." He had caught my words about part of us going to be with God and part of us going into the grave. Since the casket view only showed the top of daddy's body, Dereck's young mind conjectured that the feet must be the part that goes to heaven.

How do we as Christian parents put the mystical concept of the soul into child's language? How can we explain our firm hope in immortality so that our child doesn't come up against an unresolvable contradiction when he sees death? Can we give our child the belief of "going to God" and yet be completely honest about the finality of physical death and the pain of separation that death brings into our lives?

I think we must! Somehow we must suggest the concept of "the real me" who lives inside my body. I could allow Chad and Dereck to see Rog's body only after we had spent time talking about both the reality of death and the hope of immortality. Exposing a child to a death situation when he has only been told the religious hope of death and never informed about what happens to the body is unjustified. As parents we forget to come down to a child's level and see how contradictory a funeral looks to him.

The words we use to talk about death can be confusing to a child. As a person who believes in being straightforward and realistic in my terminology, I've gone along with those who say we shouldn't shroud death in beautiful language. When asked, I always answer, "My husband is dead," and avoid using terms like "He passed away" or "He passed over." However, for a child who is trying to learn the Christian concept of the eternal spirit, such bluntly completely materialistic statements as "He is dead" may seem a denial of what he has been taught.

When Chad came running down the hall asking, "Is daddy going to be all right?" I wanted him to grasp the whole situation as I believed it to be. Instead of saying only, "No, Daddy is dead" or "No, Daddy went to be with Jesus

49

now," I tried to combine the two as taught by the Christian faith. I said, "Daddy's body was too sick to live here. The part of daddy that we love is with God now."

I repeated that concept often during the three days of the funeral preparation. I told them that Rog would never come back because there is no way to be here without a live body. I said, "The reason I'm crying is that I didn't want him to die because I loved him so much and wanted him to live here with us." Before I took them to the funeral home I told them again, "Now we're going to see daddy's body which is dead. It can't breathe or ever move again. But remember, the part of Daddy that cared for us is taken care of by God now." Viewing Rog's body was de-emphasized by spending time looking at all the flowers and talking about the many people who loved him.

Getting a child to distinguish between the "I" who thinks and feels and chooses and the body which breathes, runs, and gets hurt is difficult. Using theological terms such as "soul" or "spirit" often seems to conjure up Halloween images of spooks and other assorted mysterious pictures in a young child's mind. To say, "Our soul goes to Jesus," may suggest a heart-shaped blob floating out of our bodies. To say, "Our spirit goes to be with the Lord," often causes the child to see a spooky, shadowy body which separates from the person.

Using the concept of the "real me" seems to cause less misunderstanding because there are fewer preconceptions surrounding the term.

Comparing the body to a house, which is empty and lifeless when the family moves out, or to a suit of clothing which just lies there until we give it life, may help.

It's surprising how many children and even teenagers have never thought about the reality of their being and how it is distinguishable from their body. After sharing such thoughts with a group of attentive teenagers, I was told by one of the parents, "I don't know what you said, but my son told me that for the first time in his life he isn't afraid to die."

The following is a puppet skit I've found helpful in explaining death to groups of children. The teacher will need a glove. Another person should take the part of Jerry who speaks from a puppet box or stage. Where questions are asked, give the children time to respond.

PUPPET SKIT FOR CHILDREN

Teacher: (Gives introduction of self and other pleasantries. After introducing Jerry, he fails to appear from his puppet box. Finally after calls, knocking, and wondering where he is, he jumps out when my back is turned.)

Jerry: Got ya! (Laugh) Boy, I really scared you that time, didn't I?

Teacher: You certainly did! (Lecture Jerry a bit on his behavior and manners.)

Jerry: Right! I didn't mean to embarrass you. Are these all the students you told me about . . .(Says "Hi" to boys and and girls, compliments them on their intelligence, and tells a joke of some sort.)

Teacher: Goodness, Jerry. You certainly are in a good mood tonight. The last time we talked you were quite sad.

Jerry: Yeah. You were telling me the story of the way Jesus died on the cross. You told me how much Jesus loves everyone no matter who they are. Jesus was God's Son and I just don't see why He had to die on that cross with those other men who were thieves.

Teacher: But Jerry, Jesus died on the cross so that we could know how to love God better. Long ago people built big altars and burned sacrifices to tell God they were sorry about something. Since Jesus died, you and I and anyone who loves God can pray anywhere. We can go directly to God and Jesus to say how much we love them or to ask to be forgiven. Besides the story doesn't end there.

Jerry: Yeah. I read that they took Him off the cross and put Him in a tomb. The soldiers rolled a big stone over the door and stood guard. Then later all those people came to the grave and an angel told them that Jesus was gone. That's the spooky part!

Teacher: Jerry, that's the happy part. It means that Jesus lives forever.

Jerry: What do you mean? If He's alive, why can't I see Him?

Teacher: Jesus ascended into God's presence. Through His Spirit He can be everywhere. What makes it even better is that Jesus gave us a great promise about our lives. Do you remember John 3:16? (Jerry leads group in reciting verse.)

Jerry: But what does everlasting mean?

Teacher: (Children give answers.) Jerry, it means forever, never ending.

Jerry: Hold it! Wait a minute! You must think I'm some kind of dummy! If people who believe in Jesus can live forever like that verse says, where are all the two-thousand-year-old people?

Teacher: The reason you don't see any two-thousand-year-old people running around is that it isn't our bodies that live forever. Our bodies die! It's our souls or spirits that live forever.

Jerry: What's a soul, a spirit? That's sounding spooky again!

Teacher: We might say that the soul is the "real you" that lives inside. It's the part of you that thinks, feels, loves, and tells your body what to do. Let me explain with this glove. Each of us is born with a body. (Put on glove.) We move, get hungry, grow, run, and play. Who were you when you were born? When 3? when 6? Who will you be when 16? when 40? when 80? You'll still be the same person no matter what your body looks like!

Jerry: You mean my grandma is the same person even if her body is old and wrinkled?

Teacher: Right! We see the outside of a person. We say, "He's smart, he's a good ballplayer, or she's the best skater." But the most important part is what kind of a person we are—how we really feel inside.

Jerry: You mean I might look nice on the outside, have a real handsome body, and still be kind of mean inside? Or I might not be much to look at, but boy do I have a good personality.

Teacher: You're catching on, Jerry. The "real you" doesn't depend on what your body looks like. For example, who would you be if your leg were cut off? What if you lost all your hair? Would you still be the same person?

Jerry: Of course. The "real me" would still be the same.

Teacher: A lot of things can happen to the body. Sometimes things happen that can't be helped. Sometimes our bodies have accidents. Usually they can be fixed, but sometimes (tear glove) they are harmed beyond repair. Sometimes bodies get a disease. Today many illnesses can be cured. For that we're grateful. Sometimes a disease gets so bad that the organs of the body can't work or the person can no longer breathe. Usually our bodies just keep getting older and older until they finally get so worn out they can't function any more.

Jerry: A lot can happen to the body!

Teacher: When things happen that can't be changed, the body dies. (Take off glove, putting that hand behind back. Holding the glove in the other hand ask . . .) Can the body move? run? play? get hungry anymore?

Jerry: No it can't do anything by itself.

Teacher: What do we do with a body when it dies? We have a funeral and we put the body in the grave. (Lay down glove). We're sad because that person is gone from us. We can't see him or play with him anymore. Being separated from someone we love is hard. We wish he could still be here with us. We cry a lot. We needed that person very much. We certainly didn't want him to die!

Jerry: When my grandpa died, I hated it. He was so nice to me and I'll never get to sit on his lap again. I still cry sometimes when I think how much I miss him.

Teacher: Jerry, do you remember what God promised about living forever? The part that made the glove move and enjoy life (bring hand from behind back) is still there. The part that is the "real you," the part you can't see, but the part that loves, cares, and feels is taken care of by God. Somehow—in a way we don't understand—the "real you" goes on living and goes to be where God's love is.

Jerry: You mean that when I die, it's my body that stops living? The real Jerry will be taken care of by God? . . . I have one problem though. Will heaven be fun? I'd sure hate to give up baseball practice, swimming, and all that fun stuff.

Teacher: All we know is that Jesus promised it would be great to be with Him. We hope all of our bodies stay healthy and that no accidents happen so that everyone here can live on earth for many years. God wants us to have a good life. However, it is nice to know that if death does happen to us or to someone we love, God is right there to take us—the "real part" of us—to be with Him.

Jerry: I think I'm going to sleep better tonight. I didn't understand about the "real me" before.

8
But My Child
Asks Such Hard
Questions

"But my child asks such hard questions," you say. "He's not content to know that the body dies. He'll want all the facts. He'll want to know how long the body keeps its form, whether the hair and fingernails keep growing, and why we have beautiful caskets if the body just decays anyway." He may have grasped the concept of the "real me." But you say, "That hardly satisfies is questions about how we leave the body, what heaven is like, and whether he'll enjoy being there."

How uncomplicated it would be to pacify his questioning with the blanket statement, "Don't worry, God will take care of everything." After all that's the best answer, isn't it? Having gone through so much searching, I find a great deal of comfort in those words. However, I certainly understand the inquisitiveness of a child. Death is such a fascinating, scary, uneasy thing to him. Over the years he has to probe, to imagine, and to ask hard questions to arrive at concepts he can believe.

Even more than needing all the right answers, our child needs to feel comfortable expressing questions without feeling ridiculous or being put down for having such thoughts. As a parent, I want my child to feel that nothing about death is unmentionable. Anything he thinks about can be expressed without fear.

I also want him to understand that I don't have nearly all the answers. Often I will say, "I don't know." But if I say, "That's an interesting question. It's something to think about," or "Let's try to find an answer," I keep the conversation open. Keeping the discussion free provides concrete chances to share my faith with him. Only if I listen to his many and difficult questions do I have the chance ultimately to be listened to when I say, "For many of our concerns, we must simply trust God."

The following questions are a sample of the kind children ask. Some are those Chad and Dereck have asked. Some come from other children. When we consider such questions with our child, we should be careful about giving absolute, specific answers simply because we want to appease our child's curiosity. I feel much more comfortable giving Chad and Dereck general responses to immortality and the afterlife than I do giving them specific answers which may be satisfying to them now but likely rejected later.

The following are samples of general impressions I have tried to give Chad and Dereck. The language and depth of thought will depend on the child's age.

What is heaven like? Most children who have had some sort of religious training have gained some idea of the afterlife. Death is accepted as "going to heaven," so a child is very curious about what heaven will be like.

The younger child easily accepts death as "being with Jesus" or "being taken care of by God." He usually has loving thoughts of Jesus and readily identifies God's love with parental love. He doesn't think much more about heaven once he has been told that "he will be cared for." Instead of mommy and daddy, God will provide for him.

Seeing heaven as being in God's love really is a vital point of Christianity. More than anything else, I want Chad and Dereck to consider immortality as continuing to know God's love. Unfortunately this simple but profound view of the afterlife is too often marred by making heaven a *place* rather than a *condition*.

As a child gets older, he begins to see himself in relation to his world. He realizes that death will separate him from what he knows here. The unknown aspects and vague concepts about God's love may not seem acceptable. As he becomes more rational, he finds it harder and harder to imagine anything that he can't see, touch, or experience.

He may become persistent in wanting a complete picture of what heaven is like. he may insist on a comparison with what he knows on earth. If we've portrayed heaven as a place, he feels he has a right to a material description. He'd like to hear us say it will be a candy-coated mountain, a glass city of perpetual riches, or a huge Disney-like land in the sky where he will never get bored. As parents it is easy to feed our child's fantasies and agree with whatever picture he draws.

Even as adults we take our own pet hobbies and beautiful aspects of life and project them into heaven so that it becomes a mere duplication of the best of earth except that sin is removed. For me heaven *should* be beautiful scenery, greenery, and waterfalls. But I know that by giving a child a material concept of heaven, I am not really being honest.

Instead I must give him a basic feel for the spiritual and for God's love so that someday he will come to the point when he can accept realities that cannot be seen. The things we see are temporal, but God's love, truth, and soul beauty are permanent. I can try to help my child understand that nothing is more important than love. The best way of doing this is letting him see that I value people and their feelings much more highly than I do material things. If he knows that my parental love will endure through any trial, he can project that God's love cannot be destroyed by anything either. Mentioning magnets and wind as examples may help the young child understand that not everything has to be visible and material to be real.

What will we do in heaven? For adults, who

can somewhat comprehend that what we *are* is more important than what we *do*, immortality can be seen as a growth in being. Getting that idea across to a child, who is the essence of *doing*, is extremely difficult.

The young child will want heaven to be a place for running, swinging, and having fun. When he asks, "Will I have a sandbox to play in and a bicycle to ride?" it seems cruel to give a definite "no." One little boy was very upset about heaven when his mom insisted that his dog wouldn't be there to play with. Yet to agree with our child that "Yes, you will do all those things in heaven" seems dishonest too.

When Dereck asked about having his bike in heaven, I felt comfortable giving him a general feeling. I said something like, "Hmm. . . . You think that would be nice? Bike riding is pretty important to you? I'm sure God has plenty of ideas that will make you happy. But being with God will be the best of all."

How do we get there? If we talk about heaven as a place and as being "up there," our child will certainly want to know by what kind of magical logistics God plans to get us there. If the child is old enough to know about galaxies and space travel, he knows that if it's up there, it has to be a long way off. How in the world is God going to get us there?

If instead we talk about heaven as a condition and see God's love as being here and everywhere instead of "up there somewhere," we avoid some of the confusion. I've tried to be careful not to talk about "Daddy being *up there* with God" so that later when I want to share the idea of dimensions, transitions, and a higher plane the boys won't think I'm talking about physical directions. I've only begun to give the boys a base for this concept. They are still physical and direction oriented. For their age, I can only begin. For instance, here's a conversation I had with Chad when he was nine years old:

"What happens when we die?" I asked to draw him out.

Chad: "Our soul goes to heaven and our body stays on earth."

"What is the soul?"

Chad: "A living thing that never dies . . . no it's not a thing. It's our heart . . . well, no, not our heart. It's part of me. . . . It's me."

"How do you 'go to heaven' like you said?"

Chad: "God takes me out . . . up? I don't know."

Perhaps the best we can do is convey the idea that nothing—not even death—can separate us from God's love. The change that occurs at death can only be left to Him. None of our verbal concepts or thought images seem appropriate for a child. Explanations of being "carried by the angels," as stated in Luke 16:22, create for the child physical pictures of white robes, wings, and halos which do not adequately convey the spiritual quality of death.

Will we know each other? Family relationships are important to a child. He wants the security of believing that we will know each other after death. The Bible seems to indicate that there will be some kind of knowing. Many cite the transfiguration story in Matthew 17:1-9, when the disciples immediately recognized Moses and Elijah, to support this idea.

Yet as adults we understand that our awareness of each other will be different from what it is here. The relationships will be changed. We envision a communication of unhindered spiritual depth and meaning.

When Chad asked if he'll know his dad, I felt comfortable saying, "We're not sure how it will be. We'll probably know each other, but it will be different from here—even better than the way we understand each other now."

As a base, we can help our child understand that we sometimes know people by their qualities and characteristics quite apart from their physical beings. We say things like, "Isn't that just like him" or "That's just the way she is." There are many ways of knowing each other and the best is saved for later.

Will we keep growing? One night as I tucked Dereck into bed, he said, "If I don't die before I'm twenty-nine, I'll be older than daddy, won't I? Or does he keep growing in heaven?" Chad immediately volunteered, "People don't have bodies there, so how can he grow?"

After they discussed it awhile—listening solves a good many problems—I said something general about "growing" not being physical as we think of it now. But that learning is a form of growing, so maybe that is how we grow in heaven. Perhaps I've opened them to a later understanding of continued soul growth and stages of awareness—exciting possibilities.

Can Daddy see us if he is with God? Chad and Dereck were sure that Rog had the same "seeing" that God has. Being with God should bring with it the same omniscience that we attribute to God, shouldn't it?

After letting them talk a long time, I found that I didn't really have to answer this one definitely. We talked about both possibilities and said something about Daddy being here through memories. They accepted my, "I don't know" because we went on and talked about "If Daddy could see us, he would be happy about. . . ." The question was mainly prompted by a wish to stay connected with their father.

How long is forever? Helping a child begin to understand time, timelessness, and eternity exceeds my capabilities. For someone as "time-bound" and "planning" as I, giving a child the concept of eternity being without time, as we know it, is extremely difficult. Chad and Dereck aren't time conscious enough to push for a long discussion. They've accepted the idea of never ending as a long, long time.

What happens to the body in the grave? Chad has just started to be interested in what happens to the body. Dereck hasn't thought about it yet. Chad knows it decays and eventually "disintegrates," as he says, but he's starting to want to know more. Recently he asked me about Washington's grave. Other students were talking about digging up the grave and seeing how he really looked. Chad said, "I told some of them that he'd be disintegrated, but some didn't even know that they put him in a casket."

For the older child an explanation of the biological aspects of death—the heart stops, blood no longer circulates, cells begin to die—may help in facing the reality of death. He may find it interesting that the brain cells usually die first and that hair may grow for several hours after death. He may want to know that embalming means removing body liquids and adding chemicals which preserve the color and form of the body for the funeral days. He has probably had enough contact with skeletons to understand that eventually the body decays.

If we are matter-of-fact about such details—which is a bit hard when we're talking about a body which we personally loved—and do not feel that the whole subject is grotesque, we can possibly convey that the body has really lost its value to us. We care much more about the essence of the person.

Why do we have caskets and bury the body? When we were having our discussion about Washington's grave, Chad and I had the following conversation about caskets.

"Why do we put dead people in caskets?" I asked.

Chad: "So we can remember them longer?"

"You mean like your friends said, so we can dig them up and see them?"

Chad: "No, just so they stay longer and don't disintegrate for 100 years or so."

"Why do we want to keep them that long?"

Chad: "I don't know. Why *do* we have caskets?"

"Could it be to remember them—like you

said—during the funeral and to show respect. Even though we don't consider the 'real person' to be part of the body anymore, it would seem disrespectful just to toss the body aside."

Chad: "Yeah."

I'm certainly not justifying the huge expense we spend on displaying and preserving the body. We could find meaning in a bit more realistic expressions of our beliefs. However the qualities of respect seem important.

Why do we have a funeral? I told Chad and Dereck that the funeral was a time for all the people who cared about Rog to come together to think about his life. We are very important to each other. When we die, those who loved us want to show their love by stopping their daily routine and saying that they are sad about our death.

The funeral also was a time for our friends and relatives to come and help us through the hard situation. They wanted to tell the family that they cared about us. They were sad because we no longer had a daddy to be with us. They told us they would stick by us and help us get along without him.

I'm sure your child has his own unique questions that require discussion. If we can keep communication open and avoid giving specific, detailed, materialistic answers, then our child's inquisitiveness can be interesting and even stimulating—a chance for growing and broadening our own concepts.

9
Concepts About Death
I Wouldn't Use
with a Child

As I periodically helped Chad and Dereck grasp the meaning of the foreverness of the "real me" and attempted to answer their specific questions about immortality, I became aware of the importance of our sharing. The concepts about death, which they heard me voice or which they saw me act out in my life, were greatly influencing their feelings about God and about the security of our continued life.

I became conscious of several concepts about death which I didn't want Chad and Dereck to catch. As an adult, I could handle certain statements because I had formulated what I believed. However, some of our adult assertions about death can cause a great deal of harm for a child who doesn't have the mental capacity to understand. Perhaps we need to reevaluate some of our statements from a child's viewpoint.

As a parent who is explaining death to a child, I would never equate death with sleeping. I have heard adults thoughtlessly tell a child, "Grandma went to sleep forever. She won't wake up till she gets to heaven." Any adult who would suggest to a child that death is sleeping has never soothed a child's fears on a dark, lonely night or held a child who doesn't want to sleep because of bad dreams. A child has enough normal problems with darkness and nighttime without giving him the idea that sleeping may mean death.

Chad and Dereck experienced their strongest feelings at bedtime. As I tucked Dereck into bed, he often cried for his daddy. Chad would react by covering his ears. He didn't want to think about Daddy right before sleeping because he might dream about him. Bedtime was an extremely painful time for many months. I can't imagine how I would have handled the added strain if Chad and Dereck had been afraid to go to sleep because some adult had unwittingly told them, "When someone dies, they're just sleeping."

If your child has had a close experience with death and is exhibiting an unusual refusal to go to sleep, make sure he understands that sleeping and death are not the same. Even though you've never given him that idea, he may have picked up the concept by overhearing adults talk about "those who sleep in Jesus" (1 Thessalonians 4:14). He may have a nagging fear that one of these times he won't be able to wake from sleep and that he'll be dead.

Not only does the thought of death as sleeping

cause fear in the child, but it also gives him a boring picture of immortality. Several biblical passages do talk about death as sleeping or "resting in the Lord." As an adult I can understand that such terms speak mainly of our soul peace. Resting is symbolic of an absence of spiritual frustration and a complete trust because our being-center is connected with Christ. However, a child certainly cannot project anything vital from the words "sleep" and "rest." What child wants to spend eternity resting?

Sleeping is too nearly synonymous with oblivion to give our child an accurate feel for immortality. Even as an adult, I have a difficult time with the feeling I get as I stand by the grave during the burial service and hear the minister read 1 Thessalonians 4:13-16. The minister always seems to emphasize the hope which the passage gives concerning "those which are asleep"; they will rise first when Christ returns. As I'm standing there I always get a sick feeling that the minister is contradicting all the things he has said about the immediacy and the gloriousness of immortality. It sounds as if he is saying, "Here in the grave the person will sleep until the resurrection." I always want to interrupt by calling attention to verse 14 which says, "For since we believe that Jesus died and rose again, even so through Jesus, God will *bring with him* those who have fallen asleep." Death does not break our relationship with Christ. To talk about sleeping or oblivion to a child creates a concept of separation from God which is not taught by the Christian faith.

Other concepts can also be harmful for a child faced with a death situation. Some parents who cannot face the thought of talking about death with the child avoid the whole thing by saying, "He had to go away" or "Grandma went on a long journey." To equate death with "going on a journey" opens up the possibilities for the child to have all kinds of bitter feelings.

First of all, he may feel abandoned by the dead person. A child often views adults as omnipotent, so he will assume that the person freely chose to go on the journey. The person deliberately left him behind. If I had told Dereck and Chad, "Daddy needed to go away," and had not allowed them to experience the whole death reality, I would have given them good reason to feel angry toward Rog. Instead they needed to be assured often that daddy did not choose to die; the disease caused his death. They needed to be reminded how much he loved them and how much he enjoyed being here with them.

Some parents say, "But I wanted my child to remember the dead person as he was when he was living. It would have been too hard on my child to know that someone he loved so much died. I couldn't think of anything to say except that he had to go away." The feeling of rejection ("He went away; he must not have loved us much anymore") and the feelings of anger ("He didn't even love me enough to say good-bye") are more traumatic feelings to deal with than knowing that death can't be helped. A child can better cope with the reality of death than with the added stress of feeling abandoned too. When he gets older he will also have to deal with the disillusionment caused by the discovery that he has been misled.

We must be aware of the effect that our adult statements have on a child. When he asks those hard questions, let's be conscious of what our concepts appear to say to him. Soon after we had buried Rog, Chad and Dereck began asking the most difficult question of all. One painful evening as I was getting them ready for bed, Chad sobbed the words, "*Why* did Daddy have to die, anyway?" Dereck's small voice joined in with, "I want Daddy here. Why did he die?"

That "why" question was repeated often during the next several months. It's a question that arises out of great heartbreak and loneliness for the person who is gone. All of us who face the finality of separation and the reality that a good, beautiful part of life is ended ask, "Why?" Why did Rog who had such an energetic, optimistic spirit have to give in to a disease that destroyed his body? He had so much to offer. Why did he die when others are allowed to live long, sometimes meaningless lives of ingratitude? It just wasn't fair that someone with his zest for life's challenges had to die so young. Why can't we each be guaranteed our 80 years on earth? My quiet but desperate adult questions which ate away at my spirit were echoed in my children's vocal concern, "But why, Mommy?"

The way we answer those "why" questions definitely provides positive or negative reinforcement in the development of our child's concept of God. One negative approach I've heard parents use in explaining the why of death to their children is to say, "Jesus needed" the person. One little girl was told regarding the death of her young brother, "Jesus loved little boys so much that He needed him in heaven."

I tremble to contemplate what that thought does to a child. Certainly the child will feel angry at Jesus for taking away someone he loved. A friend's child said regarding the death of his grandfather, "When I see Jesus, I'm going to punch him in the nose." Such feelings of anger carry over into adulthood and become real barriers to ever coming to a meaningful relationship with Christ. Had I given Chad and Dereck that reason for Rog's death, I know they would have reacted with spiteful feelings—and rightly so. They would have pleaded, "But we need Daddy too. Jesus must be mean to say He needs Daddy. Why couldn't He wait until Daddy was old before He took Him away from us?"

I wanted Chad and Dereck to have good feelings about Jesus—to see Him as a Friend. Never would I want them to think that Jesus planned the death because He needed their daddy. Rather I want the boys to see Christ as lovingly standing by when death happens; as being right there to take care of Rog when his body stopped breathing, but certainly not causing the death because "Jesus loves him so much that He couldn't wait to take Rog to heaven." That kind of love isn't very appealing to sad, unhappy little boys who no longer have a father.

The most common and perhaps most harmful concept which adults toss around readily during a time of death crisis are the words, "It was God's will." Many well-meaning Christians gently nod their heads with a "but we must look at this death as the will of God" assent. They say it so confidently, as if that pious-sounding phrase could wipe out all the pain and miraculously cause the bereaved child to accept without difficulty the end of a very special love.

How can a child possibly deal with the image of a God who willed the death of someone he loved so much? A child's mind can hardly differentiate between the causing will and the permissive will which we as adults understand to be inclusive in the term. In a child's understanding, "God willed" can only come up meaning "God wanted" or "God caused." A God who would do that deserves to be hated. Although a child is often afraid to verbalize his feelings, he may view God as an enemy of giant proportions. One little boy who was told that his brother's death was "the will of God" finally expressed his bitterness when he said, "I hate God because I had only one brother to play with and God took him away!"

Even as an adult I have a hard time understanding what is meant by those who see everything that happens as God's will. Much of what occurs on earth seems far removed from the plan of God. To lump every problem, tragedy, and experience under the all-encompassing blanket of God's will seems to disregard individual responsibility and choice as well as to overlook sin and circumstance as being causes of many situations.

When a child hears the words, "It was just his

time to go; God knows best," his young mind can only conclude that God is to blame. A driver is killed when his car crashes into a tree, a train hits a man who didn't consider the flashing lights, or a boat tips and one of the lads doesn't make it to shore. And, we tell our child, "It was God's will." Why does God get blamed for man's carelessness? The child wonders, "Does God plan accidents?"

A mother succumbs to cancer or a brother dies from leukemia and the child is told, "We must accept it as God's plan." Why does God have to be the culprit? Why do we direct the child's anger away from the disease and place it onto God? A hurricane rips through the town killing many people or a tornado strikes a village leaving members of a family dead. A child hears adults talking about "an act of God" and he concludes, "God sent the storm that killed; therefore, God is bad."

I don't want Chad and Dereck to see God as some merciless King sitting on His throne causing tragedy and suffering in their lives. Never would I give them the concept that Rog's muscular dystrophy and his death were related to the will of God. I just couldn't give them the chance to blame God for taking away their father. That concept might destroy their view of God as a loving Father. Then they would not only have lost their earthly father but would have become alienated from their heavenly Father as well.

I'd much prefer that my boys think of accidents, disease, and acts of nature simply as things that happen which can't always be helped.

Instead of giving them the possibility of blaming God, I would much rather stress that in any kind of tragedy God is standing by with love. I want them to believe that God doesn't cause death, but that He cares deeply and is right there to take care of us when we die. God doesn't send disaster, but He is readily available to help us go through difficult times.

As an adult I can become excited about the will of God because I see it as a perfect plan which desires each person to be in harmony with His love. But as long as I'm in the world, I'll be faced with problems. That's just part of the human condition. "In the world you have tribulation; but be of good cheer, I have overcome the world" (John 16:33).

What is so fantastic is that Christ helps us to overcome tragedy. He invites us to rest in His great love—to make choices, use opportunities that He gives, and accept situations to grow toward more harmony with Him. When I do that then I can truly say, "This is the will of God." Tragedy can become good if I allow suffering to mold and mellow my character, bringing me closer to God—and *that* is His will.

As adults we may find great comfort and assurance in some of our concepts about death. Let's be aware that some of these are too far above the maturity level of a child. We may be taking the risk that our child will completely misunderstand and draw unhappy conclusions about God and the total religious experience.

10
Helping a Child
When Death
Occurs

Death usually comes as a shock. Even if we are aware that death is imminent because of terminal illness or old age, we are always dazed and stunned when death becomes reality. Hopefully the explanations and concepts about death have been given before the emotional strain of a death crisis. Those beliefs we've shared will be recalled and provide a necessary base for coping.

However, as the reality of personal loss comes crashing down upon our hearts, we realize that the verbal concepts we've used to shape our child's understanding of death in no way compare to the "knowing" which he now experiences. Although we're grateful for our past sharing, all that now seems cold, intellectual recitation. Talking about death when only our minds are involved—something we know we should do—is vastly different from experiencing death with our hearts—a situation we immediately learn is more painful and heavy than we ever imagined.

Helping a child cope with a death loss is terribly demanding, especially if that death is so immediate that the child's whole world has drastically changed. For parents to think about ways they hope to help and ways they want the child to be or not to be included before death occurs seems wise. I have learned that when we're suddenly involved in a death crisis, our minds are confused by the commotion, the intensity of feelings, and the raw emotions of grief. Unless we've thought of how we want our child to be involved, we can easily ignore him and later regret the hasty and blind decisions that affect him.

Usually children are just thoughtlessly ignored when death happens. Almost immediately after hearing the news, the children see the house filled with neighbors, relatives, and friends. The adults are crying and embracing. Too often the only concern given the children involves such things as "How can we keep them occupied so they won't bother us?" or "Who will volunteer to take the children?" Often before they know what is happening, the children are whisked away from the death situation.

We were in a motel room 400 miles from home when Rog died. Those people back home who cared about us felt that was the worst possible way to face death. I'm sure they said in worried tones, "Isn't it awful that Janette is all alone with the boys." However, as I look back, I see that the four hours we waited for the private plane to come get us were important in helping us face the reality of Rog's death.

The boys and I cried together. We clung to each other. We repeated over and over the fact that the death had really happened, trying to get our uncomprehending minds to understand. Chad responded well beyond his six years and lovingly wanted to pack all of Daddy's things himself. As he folded each shirt and laid it gently in the suitcase, he quietly began to ask the many questions that played in his young mind. "Why didn't the doctors help Daddy?" he wondered. "Who will help take care of us if Daddy can't?" and "You mean I'll never have a Daddy again?"

Dereck sobbed long and hard. He really couldn't believe that Daddy would no longer be there to be with him. His tearful, I-want-daddy pleas had to be soothed with loving words. I'm glad I had time to listen to Chad and Dereck's questions and to hold them in the comfort and security of my arms.

In retrospect I see that several other good things happened during those first hours that we shared alone. First, I carefully told the boys the facts of Rog's death. I reminded them about how tired Rog had been recently and told them about the muscle disease which made it hard for him to breathe. I told them that Daddy must have been very ill inside and that his body just couldn't live anymore. I couldn't be more specific at that point because I wasn't sure what the autopsy would reveal as the cause of death.

They didn't comprehend much of what I said,

but to hear a calm, rational explanation of the death seemed good for them. A child shouldn't be subjected to gory or scary details that would frighten him, but a reasonable explanation of the death is justified. In this way he doesn't fear that things are being hidden from him or face all sorts of horrible imaginations. Giving the cause of death also keeps the child from worrying needlessly that people "drop dead" without a cause. However, in giving information we should be sure that our child doesn't begin to associate all sickness, all accidents, or all injuries with death. We certainly don't want him to fear death every time he gets sick, scratched, or bruised.

A second good thing about our time alone as a family was that it gave me a chance to reaffirm the religious hope of death. As I repeated the idea about his daddy's body dying, but God taking care of Rog, Chad seemed to grasp some of the power of that belief and its personal meaning for us now.

During those hours, God seemed to surround me with a peace and security which is indescribable. Eternity somehow touched our motel room. Beyond all doubt I knew that death meant moving to a higher plain of existence. I had not left Rog back at the hospital; he was already with Christ. A security and even a kind of excitement were given to me. It wasn't my normal nor continued reaction to death but it was real at that time.

My confidence in God and immortality was obvious to Chad and Dereck. Even though Dereck couldn't possibly understand the concept, he could feel that things were secure and that God's love was with us. Many people have told me they were also given a deeply religious experience during a death. This should be shared with our children. If they are removed and kept separated during this time of spiritual assurance, they miss a lot of insight about death.

Along with sharing in my hope concerning Rog's death, being alone in a motel room for four hours made it necessary for the boys to see my grief as well. There was nowhere to run for privacy—to protect them from seeing Mommy break down in hard tears. Seeing me cry and hearing me express feelings of terrible loss and heartbreak allowed Chad and Dereck to understand that we were all in this hurting thing together. Sometimes we just cried together as a group. Other times they took the role of comforter and consoled me as I had done them. They said, "Mommy we'll help each other. It will be okay."

Certainly children should not be subjected to hysterical displays and adults who completely lose control of themselves. But death seems like such a senseless, uncontrolled thing that emotions of helplessness, hopelessness, sorrow, and anger are natural. I tend to think that it is better for a child to see adults reacting honestly to death than to see adults smothering all their feelings and stoically acting as if the death were of no consequence. If the child is shoved out and not allowed to share in any grief, he is left to ponder all of his feelings alone. He thinks he is the only one who feels a great emptiness and concern.

Our good intentions of protecting him from our grief often leave him feeling lonely and excluded.

We must take into account the suffering of the child. Hearing grief expressed and being allowed to express his own sorrow is much more healing than isolation from reality. Sending a child off somewhere for three days while we mourn doesn't take into account that he will have strong feelings of loss to deal with too. Keeping him constantly busy and occupied so he won't think about the death is like saying, "Your feelings aren't important." Avoiding his questions by always sending him off to play says, "You're just a child. How you feel about death doesn't matter." The worst thing we can do is to refuse a child normal modes of grief by saying, "Don't cry. You must be brave."

Allowing a child to express feelings is one thing, but urging him to display unfelt emotions is quite another matter. We only make him feel guilty with questions like, "Why aren't you crying? Don't you miss Grandpa?" Young children cannot always accept the reality of death immediately. They may not feel the loss until later during a situation where the person is conspicuously absent. The parents of a seven-year-old girl were bothered when she showed little feeling at her grandmother's funeral. At a family Christmas celebration months later they were surprised when she sobbed because she missed grandma so much. The grief was not real until then.

Children also have a sort of denial of past and future—all that matters is now. Children can forget and play normally. Although Dereck cried about Rog's death, he also went off and played, running around the room and stepping outside to watch the swimmers in the nearby pool. I couldn't believe how he could take it so hard one moment and then lightly dismiss the whole thing the next. But such fluctuation is natural; we shouldn't demand grief.

That time alone in the motel allowed me to listen to Chad and Dereck's feelings. When we returned home, we were immediately surrounded by people. I needed other adults—our parents, close relatives, and friends. An empty house would have been painful. But once I was encircled by others, I had little time to give the boys. Friends took the children so I could rest and make preparations for the funeral. I needed that time and was grateful for those who helped in that way. Chad and Dereck weren't included in any of the planning—partly because they were too young, but also because I simply did not think of involving them. To ignore them and think only of my own grief was easy. A family in grief needs surrounding support and help with the children, but if they are not allowed some time alone—at least a private time for sorrow—they miss a definite part of the healing and adjustment process.

Those four hours in the motel room also allowed us to begin a sharing which set the precedent for the openness with which we talked about Rog during the following months. Almost immediately I found myself talking about memories and stressing the good life we had enjoyed with Daddy. We recalled the fun things we had done, talked about how Rog felt about being a father. We decided that we could still feel like he was near by asking ourselves, "How would Daddy feel?" when we had to make decisions alone.

I wish I had encouraged other adults to talk with the boys about Rog. Hearing some of the things people said about their father would have been good for them. Few adults said anything at all to Chad and Dereck. In the first place, the boys weren't available and, second, most adults think that one doesn't talk about death to a child. Because I didn't take the boys to the day and evening of public visitation, there was no setting for them to hear, "I'll miss your father. He was a special friend," or "Your father was important in the business. We'll miss him." The boys seemed too young for long lines of people and the solemn, quiet atmosphere of the funeral home. That is something I would reconsider, weighing the fact that perhaps a short period of seeing and hearing the many concerned and caring people may be good for a child.

Deciding how to include a child in the rituals associated with death is a personal matter which depends on the circumstances and the age and understanding of the individual child. Children who face a close death should be included not only in the mourning process before and after, but should also attend the funeral or memorial services as well. The feeling of belonging and family closeness is good for the bereaved child.

Chad and Dereck recall some things about

Rog's funeral which create good feelings. When I had a private viewing of Rog's body with them, I read each card on all the plants and flowers and pointed out how each person was related to Rog personally or through business. They still talk about the many bouquets and say, "A lot of people cared about Daddy."

Because I didn't want to go through the emotional strain of following the casket down the long aisle of the church, we had the burial first. Chad and Dereck have no problems with going to the cemetery and enjoy taking flowers there occasionally. Although we have never made a big thing out of the grave, they like to look at the stone marker. I'm sure they didn't understand much of the memorial service which followed the burial, but they drew some good conclusions. Recently Chad asked, "Do I know a lot of people? Dad sure did. Wow, a lot of people came to his funeral. He must have had a lot of friends."

Before taking any child to a funeral, we should prepare him for what is to occur. Most children can handle the situation if they've been informed about the procedures and the meaning of a funeral. However, a sensitive, unwilling child should not be forced to attend. Such children can participate in the death experience by answering the door or phone and by doing other helpful things in the home. Taking children under three years of age to a funeral may cause more disturbance than it is worth to the child.

Helping a child understand death requires thought and planning. Generally, including seems better than isolation from sorrow.

11
A Child
Has a Grief
Process Too

The way we deal with a child's immediate needs at the time of a death sets the tone for the way we handle the process of grief during the months that follow. If we've used protection and isolation, we will probably continue with that approach. An eight-year-old girl, who had been told unreal things about her dear grandfather's death to protect her, was never given the opportunity in the years that followed to face the reality of his death. As a college student many years later, she had an uncontrollable sobbing session when she realized what all those years of avoiding the grief had done not only to her but to her relationships.

If we have honestly and openly helped our child with his questions and allowed him to grieve, we have a better chance of continuing to help him work through the loss experience. Unfortunately adults often fail to understand that a death loss requires a long process of healing even for a child. For some reason we expect the funeral to be the end of it for him. Getting "back to normal" seems to be the quickest and best way of keeping him from grief.

Because children are said to adapt so much easier than adults, we often aren't conscious that we should expect them to go through steps of grief just as we do. Children return to play and fun quickly. Too often we take their outward activity as a sign of inward acceptance. People immediately said, "Chad and Dereck are taking it so well. Children adjust so *easily*."

Although I was aware of my own problems with grief, I accepted the theory that children recuperate more quickly than adults. Neither Chad nor Dereck have very demanding personalities, so disregarding their emotional needs became easier and easier as my own grief became intolerably more heavy. Often I failed to recognize their feelings not only because I was blinded by my own sense of loss, but because I didn't *expect* them to go through some of the things they did. I had accepted the cliché, "They're only children."

Many of the emotional reactions that Chad and Dereck experienced during the first months after Rog's death are clear to me only in retrospect. Sharing my failures is not meant to be a berating of myself concerning the way I handled the situation. I did as well as I could. However, the more we understand of a child's feelings, the more we can make a conscious effort to help.

Some children don't let us know they need help because they don't know how to talk about their feelings. Dereck's pain was more obvious; he cried when he missed Daddy. Chad hid his emotions from me. Because he was more quiet and unexpressive, I assumed he was doing okay. Usually I didn't get at any of his emotional needs unless a period of unusual behavior warned me there was a problem.

The funeral days provided a kind of cushion period for the shock of Rog's death. The boys' activity kept them from realizing the awfulness of a father's death. The gathering of cousins created excitement. Playing allowed them to forget. Besides they were the center of attention. Something strange, scary, and awful had happened—and the other children were awed.

Then the funeral rituals were over. The boys returned to their normal life arena and there was nothing to keep them from comprehending the realness of the death. We buried Rog on Sunday. Monday morning when I walked into the family room, Chad flipped off the cartoons on TV and said, "I try to forget that it happened, but I can't." The cushion period was over! Chad and Dereck began to feel the ruggedness of living with the fact that Daddy would never again be here to do all those things that were so much a part of their lives.

Chad and Dereck never tried to deny Rog's death after that. Both of them accepted the knowledge that his death was final. They did not hound me with questions of "When will he come back" or statements of protest such as "My daddy will come alive again" as many young children do. However, as the impact of not having a father became clear to them, their denial took another form. Immediately they began asking when we could get a new daddy. They pleaded, "But Mom, we have to have a daddy" or "We can find someone just like him to love us."

Their readiness to replace Rog with another father upset me. I couldn't believe they felt that way so soon. I lectured about loyalty, told them they should feel fortunate they *had* a good father (not all children do, you know). I was adamant that I couldn't love anyone but Rog.

Dialogue about a new father was squelched by my refusal to listen to the need behind the plea. Because I was so hurt by their insistence on a father, I failed to realize that they were in a stage of denial. I should have understood that life without a father looked like an impossible, insecure existence. Since they knew better than to deny death—we had been so honest—they would try to deny the possibility that we might go on without a father. Instead of so quickly rejecting their suggestions, I should have drawn out the real issue. We should have talked about how we were going to try to live without Daddy.

Instead of gently helping the boys face reality, I insisted they understand we weren't going to have a dad. If I had been aware of their denial, I could have tried harder to understand instead of making their wish for a father into an unmentionable subject. Even though my own emotional condition hardly left me with positive feelings about making it without Rog, I should have discussed their insecurity and worked on ways of helping them accept the fact that our life could go on without a father.

When Chad moved beyond denial and grasped the fact that we couldn't readily go searching for a new father who would step into Rog's shoes and continue the love that death had stopped, he became quite hopeless and angry. I'm sure he saw a lifetime of being fatherless—a condition which made him disgusted. His anger usually wasn't obvious. Mainly it was just a slow, quiet sullenness which came from being unable to cope with being different from other kids. Realizing how much his world had changed made him quietly withdraw, which I hardly noticed. Then suddenly his anger would come boiling to the surface and quiet Chad's temper tantrum made me realize that all was not well.

Too often I only dealt with the bad behavior and didn't get to the reason behind the outbursts. Instead of trying to understand what was causing Chad to act so out of character, I felt I needed to show that I could control a child's behavior by myself. Fear of being a "weak widowed mother" made me suppress his anger and caused him to become even more quiet.

Chad also went through a stage of self-pity. His self-image suffered a bad blow during those weeks when he felt everything was wrong. Although he had always been reserved, Chad always had many friends. Slowly he began to feel that no one liked him at school. If anyone teased him or said something that he could take as an insult, he was hurt. Our bedtime routine became filled with what unpleasant things other children had done or said. During this time he was nicknamed "Charlie" by the other first-graders. Explaining that nicknames are fun and that he should be happy he was given such a good one took a lot of time. I told him each relative's pet name. Having him invite friends in to play and finding playmates in our housing development helped.

Not only did he think his friends had deserted him, but he also thought that I didn't want him around. For a period of time, all my discipline ended with him saying, "You don't like me, do you?" "I bet you wish I'd die too" were words hard to deal with. One evening we visited my parents. Dereck and I had been in the house for five minutes when we realized that Chad hadn't come in. After a long search, we found him crying in the garage. He finally told me, "Grandma doesn't care about me either." I slowly drew out the fact that she had held the door open for us, but that Grandma hadn't waited for Chad to get out of the car. When he saw the door close on him, his self-pity concluded that he wasn't wanted.

A major portion of the love that Chad had known had been wiped out of his young life. Those of us who were near him should have understood that we had to give much more love than before. Emotional exhaustion kept me from giving as much attention as Chad needed. I'm grateful for friends and relatives who stuck by Chad and helped pull him out of his self-pity.

Having male friends who stepped in and gave him the attention he needed helped considerably. Being surrounded by enough people who cared, finally seemed to fill some of Chad's love vacancy. A teacher and other adults who made a special effort to build his self-image gave him the push he needed to overcome his bad feelings about himself and his life.

There were other feelings that were hard to handle. Seeing an energetic child go through apathy and listlessness was difficult. Although I could sense apathy building within myself, seeing a child lose the excitement in his eyes saddened me. At times Chad didn't want to be involved in much of anything. He went through melancholy times when he wondered if we'd ever have a fun, happy family life again. He endured lonely times when he missed Rog and all the things we used to do together.

Fortunately many people were willing to help provide fun things for Chad and Dereck to do. The boys received invitations to participate in all kinds of activities. My nephew and my father built Chad a workbench for Christmas and interested him in making wooden things. Other friends helped with sports, took the boys to games, and stopped in for fun times with them. I couldn't have drawn Chad out alone because I just didn't have the energy to involve him in interesting things.

Worry is another feeling that death brought to Chad and Dereck. They became apprehensive whenever I felt ill. They worried that I would die too and they would be sent to an orphanage. I always had to explain that I simply had the flu or was tired; I wasn't going to die. They had learned at a young age that life is uncertain. Assuring them that I was in good health and telling them who would take care of them if something happened to me helped somewhat.

Recently Chad told me that one of his biggest concerns when we were first alone was that a robber would break into our home and there wouldn't be a dad to protect us from danger. He always insisted on a night-light and having the bedroom door open. Each night Chad made up many excuses for avoiding sleep—"One more drink," or "One more question," or "Mom, my leg hurts."

If we who are helping a child face death anticipate some of these reactions, we can perhaps move beyond the terrible depression of our own grief and realize that our child needs help too.

12

Adjustment Is Difficult and Frightening

Helping a child understand and deal with the feelings caused by grief must be followed with support in helping him adjust to his new environment. Eventually we hope the child can accept his new situation and find meaning in the revised patterns and structures of family life. Coming to that adjustment and acceptance is difficult and frightening. Chad and Dereck faced many adjustments during the first year after Rog's death. Dereck had fewer obvious difficulties than Chad. Adjustment seems to be harder for older children.

I agree with those who say that the environment of the bereaved child should be kept as normal as possible. Moving to a new town and a new school can bring too much added strain for a child who has just faced the death of a parent or a close sibling. Breaking ties with established friends and being forced to make new ones can be a gigantic task for the child going through grief. Moving should be considered only if the emotional benefits, such as being nearer relatives and grandparents who will give the necessary love, outweigh the negative aspects of disrupting the child's social surroundings.

The child's home environment should be kept as intact as possible. Continuing schedules and normal patterns of living helps the child adjust. Hopefully the young mother will have enough insurance, mortgage resources, and enough Social Security so she doesn't need to take a job immediately while her children need more than usual attention. A father can now draw Social Security to provide mothering and housekeeping for his children.

Maintaining basic schedules and doing things that were a normal part of family life are not easy demands. We must admit that no matter how hard we try to give our child a regular environment, our family situation has changed drastically. It can never be the same. We have to face that fact and help our child adjust to the new reality.

When a child sees that family relationships are no longer the same, he may feel that he must take a different role in the family structure. An older male child may assume that he is going to have to be the man of the family now that father is dead. A widowed mother often finds herself looking to the children for help beyond their capabilities. Grief keeps her from seeing what is happening.

Often a child who loses a mother will revert to baby tendencies to get attention and show that he needs mothering. He may maneuver a grief-stricken grandma or aunt to give him what he demands because they feel so sorry for him. Although a bereaved child needs a lot of love, he doesn't need doting pity. Spoiling him and accepting him as a baby again hardly is the answer.

A child who loses a brother or sister may try to act like that person to fill the void or because he observes how much the parents cared for the dead child. When we see our child wanting to take on roles that are unwarranted, we can help him by making his normal position in the family seem important to him.

Dependency is a common problem that arises as the bereaved child attempts to adjust to his new family situation. Before, Chad and Dereck had taken an independent approach to living. They were always happy to stay with a sitter, enjoyed going alone for overnight visits with friends, and readily entered into activity without their mom's help.

That independence helped them immensely in handling Rog's death and in giving me some time alone which I definitely needed. However, as the months went by, I noticed a change in the boys. Dereck started crying when I'd hire a sitter for the evening. Before when I left them for a weekend with grandparents they always wanted to stay longer. Now both of them worried that I might not come as soon as I said. Chad started asking me to interfere when he felt mistreated in his play with other children.

Now I see that instead of helping them overcome their change toward dependency, I may have encouraged it. The boys seemed to be the only good I had left in life. I always wanted to be near so that I could keep an eye on them. For a time I became overprotective because I worried that something might happen to take them away too. Having the boys need me was my lifeline to survival. I unconsciously held tightly, wanting them to be more dependent to prove how needed I was.

Fortunately I realized early what was happening and tried hard to raise them in the freer style which allowed more self-reliance again. Fostering dependence can be easily camouflaged as kindness. Consequently what we think may be helping a child may be "holding too close." Better solutions can be found for the bereaved child who doesn't want to sleep alone than fostering dependency by encouraging him to share our bed. If our child refuses to attend school or be out of our sight, we'd better work on the problem instead of continually writing excuses to the teacher and deciding to limit all our social activity to be with the child. Perhaps we'd better ask ourselves how much we are contributing to the distorted dependency. If we cannot find solutions, professional help may be needed.

When Rog died, Dereck was still young enough that he generally heeded my discipline. Correcting a first-grader became another matter. Chad soon began to test my authority. Unfortunately ours had been a typical house where father's voice carried more weight. Chad knew that I was frustrated by having to discipline by myself and he sometimes took advantage of the situation.

My grief often kept me from being consistent or decisive. Instead of being firm about the rules of the house, I easily became frustrated and angry when Chad didn't respect my authority the way I thought he should. Instead of helping him work out a discipline problem or understanding that he was testing his new situation, I worried only about the bad behavior and took it as an insult against my capability. Too often I either punished too quickly or threw up my hands and ignored the condition. Sometimes I just nagged until we both were unhappy.

During times when I felt strong because I made up my mind that I could raise the boys alone, things went much better. Chad seemed to need to know that there was some security in his shattered world. He wanted the love of discipline.

Simply tolerating obnoxious behavior because "the poor child has been through so much already" didn't give Chad the stability he needed. Neither did simply being tough so he'd know I was in control. We needed to work at the causes of his problems. I started to encourage him to talk and say what was bothering him instead of bottling it inside till it erupted in bad behavior.

However this talking caused another problem of adjustment with which I had a hard time coping. Because I no longer had a husband to listen to my frustration, I allowed the boys to hear more of my anger and unhappy feelings. I found myself leveling with them in no uncertain terms. I talked straight about how angry their picking on each other made me or how upsetting I found their lack of cooperation.

When Chad started expressing his frustration with me or what I was doing, I reacted strongly. We had never allowed back talk before. Although we encouraged honesty, we always expected anger and harsh feelings to be expressed calmly and rationally.

I fluctuated in knowing how to handle Chad's sudden outbursts of words. Sometimes I demanded, "You don't talk to your mother like that! You must change that tone of voice." I used punishment to correct, but I knew that Chad was right when he said, "But you talk to me that way. Why can you get mad and I can't?" Other times I'd decide to allow him to say exactly what he felt, because psychologists said that it is better for a child to talk back and express his frustration than to smother it all inside and never have honest communication. Yet when I followed that approach, I could hardly tolerate the lack of respect.

Chad was obviously unhappy with both approaches. After a lot of bad scenes, we finally seemed on the road to working it through. When I realized that Chad was modeling my actions rather than my advice, I tried hard to be more rational and less given to outbursts of my own. A child trying to adjust to a new and undesired home situation needs to have freedom to express his deepest feelings. I wanted Chad to continue to be honest, but I felt he needed to know that certain modes of expression—irrational yelling, name-calling, and harsh demanding—were not accepted. If he resorted to that, he could expect correction.

The biggest adjustment for Chad and Dereck was that they no longer had a male image against which to measure their aggression and toughness. A first-grader is a lively, moving character who thrives on physical tussling, running, and jumping. If he has a younger brother to tease and to fight, he will. For some reason I could only recall how well they had played together when Rog was living. Now it seemed everytime I entered the room, I was faced with a wrestling match or with screaming boys chasing down the hall.

Often the tussling turned to hurting and pounding which brought an upsetting reaction from me. How much of their physical fighting was normal play? How much was just mean behavior that needed to be stopped? A widowed friend, who had been counseled that some of her son's maladjustment came from the fact that he had no male tussling and physical handling, told me I should let them go to it. They needed that roughness for healthy development as boys. Other times I felt that I was permitting them to become hurting, unfeeling people by not interfering.

The adjustments of the child who has faced a sudden and unplanned alteration of his happy, secure family life structure are many. If he cannot find the support he needs to work out his problems of change, he may have to find distorted ways of coping with his new life.

13
We
Are Still
a Family

Perhaps the healthiest adjustment began to occur when I stopped attributing all of the boys' misbehavior and emotional frustrations to the effects of death on their lives. Even though all the problems connected with their loss were not solved, it was good when I could see them move on. When they nor I no longer blamed every bad day or depressing moment on the death, I knew that we were beginning to be restored—that life was returning to normal. When we finally started to accept our family and our life, I felt renewed hope.

It took Chad a good year to begin to see our family life as an acceptable unit. I'm sure the boys learned many of their reacting cues from me. My own personal grief took that long to overcome. I'm convinced that the way we work out our adult sorrow and the means we choose to cope with our situation will be modeled by our children. If we use evasive, escaping methods, our child will do the same. Only if we as parents accept the fact that certain things are necessary steps in the healing process will we be able to help our child accept his new situation. There were several things we had to do before we could honestly and convincingly say, "We are still a family."

One of the biggest barriers we had to overcome was our bondage to Rog and to the past. For so long we measured everything by how it compared to before—when Rog was living. We were constantly saying, "When Daddy was here, we did it like that" or "Since Father died, we can't. . . ." Everything "after" seemed insignificant in relation to "before." We were living in the past, thinking that the present and the future could not possibly offer anything in comparison to the joy we had known.

Good memories are a beautiful thing—sometimes the only thing that makes separation bearable. Talking about Rog made being cut off from him less abrupt. We couldn't let go immediately. Memories provided our needed connection with him. Recalling fun times, the way Rog cared, and the close feelings we had as a family was a balm to us when we could not yet face an uncertain future. By using memories in a constructive way, I felt I could make the good influence of Rog's life a positive force for the boys even if they couldn't have their father here.

Talking and recalling also did much more. It

provided a gradual release from bondage to Rog and to our past life. When the remembering was fairly realistic—not only the bliss—it helped us move beyond warped idealization. Smothering recall would have brought a morbid preoccupation that talking helped us overcome. Each time a memory was discussed, the pain became less severe.

Gradually we began to accept those times for what they were—good days, but not the only days. Talking helped us release the past to be the past. No matter how hard we wished or tried, it could not be the present. When we finally grasped that—and it took a long time and a lot of struggle—the past lost its powerful hold on us. Talking ourselves out of bondage to the past was necessary before we could accept ourselves as a family unit.

Another thing we had to do to see our family as good was to overcome the stigma under which we felt so pressured. For so long we viewed ourselves and felt that others saw us as "that poor family without a father."

Not fitting into the typical mold can be awkward and defeating to one's group concept. Dereck was too young to feel much awkwardness, but being without a father brought some embarrassing times for Chad. He didn't mind if individual friends talked about it, but he didn't want the "whole class" to know. Consequently, he continued to make valentines for both Mom and Dad, kept quiet when the class talked about fathers, and tried to ignore the fact that he didn't have a dad to coach from the sidelines in peewee baseball. He would never volunteer the fact that he didn't have a dad and only quietly admitted it if asked directly. He didn't like being different. He had a poor concept of us as a family; we were incomplete and odd.

When I saw the unhappiness and insecurity that our fractured family life had on the boys, I resolved to try extra hard to provide a good home situation. Back in the motel room during those hours after Rog's death, I had promised myself and the boys that we would still be a family. Yet, no matter how I worked at it, that vow was hard to keep.

The strength to go on and become a real family again came only after a lot of effort and much defeat. I had to remind myself continually of the commitment. Hearing Dereck sob, "We're never going to have fun without Daddy" or listening to Chad plead, "Can't you play with me the way Daddy did?" forced me to renew again and again my decision to try to restore our life as a family.

Help in overcoming the stigma of being a fatherless family was given by those who were sensitive to our feelings of needing to develop a good concept about ourselves. Chad's school-teacher understood and didn't make a big fuss about his situation or call for pity from the other children. Neither did she ignore it, which would have been cruel and unreal too. She just quietly let Chad know she cared by saying such things to him as, "Chad, you can make the Father's Day gift for your grandpa." Caring Sunday school teachers always informed me ahead about any activity that called for a man so the boys wouldn't be embarrassed at not having someone there for them.

Friends took the boys to father-son banquets, came to watch Chad play ball, and included us as if we were a normal family. They asked to do things *with* us instead of *for* us. They treated us as an equal family, not as a patronizing effort to help a poor widow and her two sons. Those who made us feel wanted and expected us to contribute to the fellowship did much for our family image. I found it hard to relate to those who befriended us with the attitude of "Let's do something for that poor family." Gradually, as I gained strength to create a stable family situation, I felt the stigma lift not only from our own minds but from the feelings of other people.

During the second year after Rog's death, I tried hard to prove to the boys that one parent was enough. By then I had gained back some of my confidence and some of my sense of humor so that I could tell the boys whenever they lamented the fact that they didn't have a dad, "But look, you have a great mother." I tried hard and succeeded much of the time in making our life as close to normal as possible. As I gained more independence and started to relax about our life, I realized how much we really enjoyed each other. The three of us began to crystalize into a real family and life became good again. As I looked at my sons, I knew they were not being deprived of anything. Nothing was different about them— except the love and care Rog would have given.

A family's concept of itself is important to any child. To determine how Chad and Dereck felt about our life now, I asked each of them the following questions "privately" as we say when we want to discuss something of concern. Their answers were revealing.

What was best about our life before Daddy died?
 D: "I can't remember much. He'd hold me."
 C: "A lot! The way we played ball."
Do you think we three make a good family?
 D: "Yes. Chad's sometimes nice. Mommy kisses me when I go to school."
 C: "Yes . . . well, yes and no."
Do you like our family as it is?
 D: "No. Daddy's not living! What do you think?"
 C: "No, sometimes I don't have anyone to play with. You have so much work and Dereck is sometimes too little."
Is our family as good as other families?
 D: "David has a dog. He's lucky."
 C: Yeah, as good as others. Some families treat kids bad.
Is it as good as before?
 D: "Of course! It's good even without a daddy."
 C: "No."
What would you change to make our family better?
 D: "I wouldn't sell Chad for $100. I wouldn't sell you for $1,000. Because I love you."
 C: "My biggest wish is to have a dad."
You don't like our family the way it is?
 D: "Yes, but with a dad I'd love it!"
 C: "Yeah, but not as much as before."

104

Do you think we're happy?

D: "Yeah, most of the time."

C: "Yes."

How can you tell?

D: "Wow! You don't know that? We got a smile on our face."

C: "We don't sit in the room and pout about Daddy dying."

Do you think you'd be happier with a dad?

D: "Yes, but I'm happy both ways."

C: "With our daddy, but I don't know about a new daddy."

What could you do with a dad that our family can't do now?

D: "He could fix things. Now we gotta go to their house and ask. With a daddy, we could just tell him."

C: "Play with him."

How do you feel at school when other kids know you don't have a father?

D: "I was going to tell them for show and tell, but they already knew."

C: "I get sick inside because I keep remembering when he died."

The boys' answers told me that thirty months after the death which so splintered their world, they feel fairly good about our family again. They see us as basically happy. Because I have tried so hard to make one parent "do" and because they have stopped pushing and pressuring for a new father, I thought they no longer felt as much of a void as their answers revealed. Dereck had gone from asking the first man he saw me date, "Are you going to marry my mom?" to statements like, "If you marry, we'd have one more person to tell us what to do." I thought Chad wasn't feeling much concern about having a father either. He seemed satisfied with his life and had told me that he knew a new father would bring changes which he may or may not like.

The wish for a father is natural and healthy. The fact that both Chad and Dereck have come to an acceptance that our life is good now has changed their insistence to wholesome wishing. Before, a new father would have been merely replacing Rog. They would have expected him to be exactly like they had known Rog to be. Chad and Dereck have learned that love cannot immediately be filled and replaced. They have had time to gain the security of making it alone. They have learned that death doesn't have to be the end for the remaining family members. Life does go on and it can be good again.

They no longer will require another father to wear Rog's shoes. They will more readily give him the freedom to have his own identity as a father. We will be free to form a new concept of a family and not insist that we follow the old patterns that we had known with Rog.

Dereck's kindergarten teacher gave him a fine compliment when she said, "Dereck is a happy, responsive boy. One would never know from his adjustment that he doesn't have a father." Chad's teachers have said much the same about him. At this point it is good to be able to say that in spite of the death of a father, we are still very much a family!

14
Can a Child
Be Prepared
for Death?

Can a child ever be prepared for death? The answer must be a quiet "no." There is no way to understand in advance all the emotional struggles and the pain that will come from the actual death of someone we love so much. Walking through the experience seems to be the only real way of learning. However, as parents we can certainly do much that will help our child face the hard reality of death.

We can overcome our parental inclination to protect our child from the knowledge of death. Death can neither be wished away nor ignored. To bury our heads in the sand or sit with our fingers crossed, hoping that our child will make it to adulthood without facing any death crisis is foolish. Explaining death before we're personally involved removes some of the strain of having to answer hard questions for the first time when we are totally immersed in our own grief.

Although children differ in their feelings and questions about death, all have death thoughts. By listening carefully and drawing out our child, we can learn what his individual needs are. If he needs security, we can let him know he's loved and surrounded by people who will take care of him. We can use natural situations to talk about death in a rational, meaningful way. Most important of all, we can give our child a solid base of knowing God's love and depending on His ability to see us through all of life. We can use death to teach our child about the meaning and preciousness of life.

As parents we must remove our own fears and problems with death from the closet, where they are secretly controlling us, and come to terms with our own feelings about death. If we haven't formulated an adult belief and concept about death, we will revert to passing on fantasies and clichés. We can decide not to provide answers to our child which we ourselves cannot accept.

Even though death will always remain vague and mysterious, talking about it with our child takes away some of the mystery and the fear which surrounds the word. When we discuss death with our child, we can try to use terms within his level of understanding. We can encourage him to ask questions and respond freely, knowing that only by listening to him do we have a chance of sharing our faith. We can be cautious about giving him detailed, specific answers regarding the afterlife which he may have to reject when he gets older. Giving a general feeling about death is more important than having all the right answers. We can be aware of how some of our adult concepts sound to him and avoid using explanations that could adversely effect our child's image of God.

Deciding ahead of time, when we are not emotionally involved, how we want to include our child during a death crisis will allow us to consider his needs rationally. Then when death comes, we will not ignore our child simply because we hadn't given death a thought before. We will make decisions according to his individuality, not because of pressure at the time of death.

The most help we can give our child in facing death is to understand that he has a grief process too. By expecting some of his emotional feelings, we can better help him through them. We can understand that adjustment to life without the love he depended on can be difficult and frightening. Knowing that, we can find ways of better handling the problems of adjustment. We can eventually lead him into a new concept of family, where he finds meaning and happiness in the present because he has overcome the bondage to the past and accepted his present situation as a good thing too.

Perhaps we can never get to the point of accepting death as part of our natural awareness. No matter how many deaths I'll face, I will always feel that death just shouldn't happen. I will never unprotestingly accept the breaking of relationships which death brings. As parents we can decide to be honest and open with our child, helping him express his deepest feelings about death. Only by being aware of his needs and fears can we hope to guide him in his understanding of death. As we accept the challenge of answering our child's questions about death, we have the opportunity to grow and learn new meaning in our own concepts of death.

Janette (Rupp) Klopfenstein grew up in the Archbold, Ohio area. She holds a BA in language arts and has taught on the high school and technical college level. She has written several articles and has shared her experience with death with many groups.

Her first book, *My Walk Through Grief* (Herald Press, 1976), concerns her personal struggle with the death of her young husband. It was written eighteen months after his death. This second book grew out of an awareness that explaining death to a child and helping him handle a death crisis are difficult tasks. *Tell Me About Death, Mommy* was written thirty months after the death.

Since the writing of this book, Janette has married Dr. L. Douglas Yoder and has moved with sons, Chad and Dereck, to West Liberty, Ohio, where Doug has a veterinary practice.